I0135411

A RAT'S NEST OF RAILS

Tundra, Ice, Mosquitoes, and Permafrost-Saga of the Alaska Railroad

STEVE LEVI

MASTER OF THE IMPOSSIBLE CRIME

PC PUBLICATION
CONSULTANTS
WE BELIEVE IN THE POWER OF AUTHORS

PO Box 221974 Anchorage, Alaska 99522-1974
books@publicationconsultants.com, www.publicationconsultants.com

ISBN Number: 978-1-63747-196-8
eBook ISBN Number: 978-1-63747-214-9

Library of Congress Number: 2023935054

Manufactured in the United States of America

CONTENTS

THE RAT'S NEST REVISITED

Today, the Alaska Railroad is the most visible rail line in the country. Though America hosts an intricate web of interconnected steel tracks from coast to coast, very few Americans can name even a dozen of the companies whose rail cars use those rail lines. In fact, if you are at a rail crossing anywhere in the Lower 48 and take stock of every one of the cargo containers which whip by, you will be stunned by the plethora of logos and names on the sides of the cars. Just because you are in Iowa does not mean all the cars on that train are from Iowa. The rail cars you will see come from all over America and are used by many different companies to deliver products from coast to coast.

Not so the Alaska Railroad.

Every Alaska Railroad convoy is not an amalgamation of box cars from various rail lines and different companies. They are all Alaska Railroad cars. This is because the Alaska Railroad is a standalone operation, the only one in America.

The root of this uniqueness comes from what *cannot* be found in the United States Constitution. Two of the most important items which other countries have in their formation documents that are lacking in ours – assuming you are an American reading this entry – are the establishment of a national bank and a national transportations system. There is no Bank of the United States. This is because the power to create banks has been left to the states and the private sector. Banks were not regulated by the Federal government until the formation of the Federal Deposit Insurance Corporation in 1933. Before that date, anyone could open a bank and many anyones did. They took in deposits, printed their own money and by and large, most of those banks went belly up.

A second item missing in the United States Constitution is the establishment of a national transportation system. That was left up to the states as well. Just like the banks, anyone could start a railroad and, again, a lot of anyones did. It would not be until the establishment of the Interstate Commerce Commission in 1887 there was any regulation of the rail lines.

Highways are the same. They are part of the national highway system established by the Federal Aid Road Act of 1916. What many people *do not know* is America's highways may be funded by the federal government but are still owned by the states. The repair and maintenance of those roads are not paid for by the United States government. Those maintenance dollars come from a national fuel tax. Every time you fill up at a gas station, 18.4 cents per gallon of gasoline and 24.4 cents per gallon of diesel fuel go into the Highway Trust Fund and it is this fund that pays for road construction and maintenance.

It is also critical to the understanding of the Alaska Railroad to note the United States Constitution specifically leaves the construction and ownership of transportation systems to the states.

But it says nothing about territories.

Thus it was legal for the federal government to build and own the Alaska Railroad because, prior to 1959, Alaska was a Territory, not a *state*. The Alaska Railroad remained federal property after Alaska became a state in 1959 but was regulated by the State of Alaska. It was not until 1985 that the railroad was legally transferred to the State of Alaska.

However, the history of the Alaska Railroad is somewhat speckled – and mind-boggling. Keeping it as simple as possible, the railroad itself was established by swallowing up bankrupt railway systems. The bankrupt railways were bought out – much to the *joy* of the shareholders of those defunct rail lines. Then, from March 12, 1914, to July 15, 1923, the Alaska Railroad was a federal project. All this being said, there are four aspects of the Alaska Railroad that are, at best, glossed over by history books.

Why there was funding in the first place?

For a moment be a hard-nosed economist and look at the dollars and cents of the construction of the railway system. The Alaska Railroad was initially funded with an appropriation of $35 million in 1912. Keeping the arithmetic as simple as possible, $35 million in 1912 has the equivalent value of $964 million in 2022. Real value would be twice that and, in comparison to labor costs today, the railroad would have cost $4 billion.

So?

Well, in 1920, midway through the construction of the Alaska Railroad, even during the summer when fishing was an Alaskan economic mainstay, Seward had a population of 652 people. Anchorage was booming with 1,856 and Fairbanks had 1,155. Can you imagine the uproar today if the federal government funded a road for **$4 billion** that would only benefit **3,663 people?!**

So why the railroad?

Actually, the answer is quite simple: the Alaska Railroad was not designed to benefit 3,663 people. It was designed to provide coal to the United States Navy. The complete answer begins in the 1890s when Admiral Alfred Thayer Mahan wrote two books on naval power. One of his advocates was Theodore Roosevelt who did two things to enhance American sea power. First, President Roosevelt – who had been Assistant Secretary of the Navy from 1896 until he resigned to command the Rough Riders in the Spanish American War in 1898 – aggressively transformed the United States Navy from a fleet of wooden ships powered by the wind to steel ships powered by steam. This did wonders for the steel industry because it suddenly had a large new customer: the United States Navy.

It also stimulated the coal industry.

But there was a problem.

At the same time the United States Navy was making the transition from wind to steam, the Pacific Ocean was opening up to America. In the days of sailing ships, cargo vessels had to travel in the direction of the blowing wind. In the Pacific, this was in a circular pattern north from Cape Horn on the southernmost tip of South America toward Southeast Asia. To reach the West Coast of North America, ships had to ride the winds north toward Japan and then east along the Aleutians before heading south to Seattle, Portland, San Francisco, Los Angeles and then down the coast of South America. But with steam, ships did not have to depend on the direction of the wind.

But they did have to depend on coal.

Thus islands in the Pacific were 'acquired' and became Naval stepping stones across the Pacific: Hawaii, Midway, Wake, Guam and the Philippines. The Panama Canal Zone was also 'acquired' and a canal built to allow cargo and Naval vessels faster access to the Pacific.

But fuel was a problem because the coal that powered Navy ships was on the East Coast and Roosevelt wanted Navy ships on the Pacific Ocean. To supply the Navy ships on the Pacific Ocean, coal had to be sent across the United States by rail. A better – and more economical alternative – was to have the coal available on the West Coast. The only place where there were available coal fields was the Territory of Alaska. And Alaska was the perfect patsy because it was federal property and the coal fields that were being mined were not owned by anyone. They were simply being worked under contract. By canceling the federal contracts, the coal fields could become naval coaling options.

Which is why the Navy was so interested in the Alaska Railroad.

WHAT'S WRONG WITH PUTTING THE ARMY IN CHARGE?

Second, if there is any one project in American history that was truly socialistic, it was the Alaska Railroad. The federal government owned it, constructed it, and managed it. It paid the workers, provided the food and lodging for the workers and decided all labor issues.

And it was a mess, the theme of this book.

For better or worse, capitalism with all its flaws is a productive system. You either make a profit or you do not. If you cannot compete, you go out of business. If someone does not want to work for you, they do not have to. You cannot stop employees from striking, forming unions or s-l-o-w-i-n-g d-o-w-n to show management how important the workers are. But in a socialist system, the government runs everything.

Which is what the Alaska Railroad did.

Worse, the United States Army was in charge. To its credit, in a crisis the United States military is perfection in motion. It has the people and command structure to 'get the job done' quickly and efficiently. But the United States military, from the ground up, does not have a capitalistic bone in its structure. What is important is the completion of an assignment, not the cost. Even more important, all workers are expected to fit into the military mold even if they are not in the military. Military justice is an oxymoron and the expression, "There is the right way, the wrong way and the Army way," has no meaning when you are building a railway over tundra under clouds of mosquitoes where the mud is knee-deep and hungry brown bears weigh 2,000 pounds and can run 35 miles an hour. Alaska is not Kansas but, to the military, Alaska is Kansas.

Socialism, prohibition and birth control are great ideas, but they won't work. Socialism is an excellent idea when it comes to public funding for roads, schools, libraries, parks, and health care. But it is a terrible idea when it comes to wages, contracts, benefits, and promotions. The Alaska Railroad started as a coal-transporting arrangement for the Navy and bumbled through almost a decade of a rat's nest of interlocking problems. It would not be until the arrival of Noel Smith of 1924 that the Alaska Railroad was transformed from a socialist nightmare into a workable public transportation entity.

WHAT WAS THE LONG GAME?

Third, one of the basic problems with the Alaska Railroad remains today. Alaska is viewed by Americans – and Congress – as a backwater of civilization. It is massive but has so few people – 600,000 in 2020 – that people in California, Texas and Ohio feel Alaska should not have two senators. To these people, Alaska is an icebox *somewhere* up north and fiddle de dee.

That's pretty much the attitude in the lower states overall. It's the product of poor education, not knowing enough to care, and not wanting to learn. Yes, while Alaska is incredibly large in area it is also incredibly small in population. But this camouflages the fact Alaska regularly gives up trillions and trillions of dollars to corporations in the lower states in the form of natural resources. These resources include gold, whale oil, coal, cod, potatoes, copper, silver, zinc, graphite, lead, salmon, crab, halibut, herring, hooligan, and fur. Alaskans get barely a fraction of a fraction of a penny of every dollar those resources earn for the companies in the Lower 48. Madison Square Gardens was funded with gold from Nome but no one in New York gives Alaska so much as a howdy-do for funding that structure.

Returning to the era of the Alaska Railroad, in November of 1917, while World War I was raging in Europe, there was a revolution in Russia. The Czar was out and the Bolsheviks, the Red Russians, were in.

Except they were not.

There was ongoing fighting between the Red Russian and the last of the Czar's followers, the Mensheviks, White Russians.

Then the Red Russians signed the Treaty of Brest-Litovsk which took Russia out of the war. This created a massive problem for the United States because one of our Allies, Czechoslovakia, had 50,000 soldiers who were now marooned in Russia. They had been fighting the Germans on the Russian Front. On the Eastern side of the conflict. Now that the Eastern Russian Front had evaporated, those 50,000 soldiers had to be evacuated along the 5,716 miles of the Trans-Siberian Railway – which was a war zone with Red Russians fighting White Russians. To 'facilitate' the evacuation of the Czech soldiers, 7,000 American soldiers were sent to Siberia.

Then things got sticky.

When the 7,000 American soldiers arrived in Siberia, they were met with 20,000 Japanese soldiers. This was a very large problem for the United States generally and the Territory of Alaska specifically. To begin, in the era of the Alaska Railroad, the Territory of Alaska was a very rich, low-hanging harvest on an international fruit tree. Alaska had enough gold, copper, coal, and fish to keep an army in the field indefinitely but no combat troops to stop an invader from taking the Territory lock, stock, cannery, and gold mine. Alaska had every possible asset for a nation at war and no army to protect those assets.

That, unfortunately, was the good news. The bad news was staggering. As soon as the First World War started, the Japanese saw a golden opportunity for expansion. Germany could not send its Navy to protect German colonies in the South Pacific, so Japan just scooped them up. Japan then, geographically, gobbled its way north into and through China and into Siberia.

The United States had sent 7,000 men into Siberia to protect the Trans-Siberian Railway, but Japan sent in 20,000 men to – so Japan said – protect Siberia.

All the way west to Lake Baikal, 1,200 miles from the Pacific Coast of Russia.

No one in Washington D. C. believed Japan was going into Siberia as a peace-keeping force. The United States Department of Defense was convinced Japan's entry into Siberia was nothing more than another naked land grab. It was expected that when the United States troops left Siberia, the Japanese would stay and colonize the former Russian Far East. It would turn Siberia into another Japanese colony.

Worse, Japan had a reputation for slaughtering non-Japanese people in their occupied territories. This blatant racism caused major problems during both World War I and World War II. We, human beings, all live on the same planet, and we have to get along with everyone else. All of us, all the time. America is a good example of different people getting along. We have our problems but, by and large, immigrants and refugees entering America 'fit in.' It takes time. Sometimes several generations. But immigrants and their descendants do not disappear. Rather, they change the American culture.

Even more important, there was a major philosophical difference between the Japanese and the Americans in this era.

Americans looked upon conquered people as the customers of tomorrow. Americans are the ultimate businesspeople. We want the world to buy our products. When World War I was over, we wanted the people of the world to buy what we produced. It was what made us wealthy. So, we wanted to save as many of the conquered people as possible. They were our meal ticket in the decades to come. Our factories were going to make things we were going to sell to them. And our factories hired Americans whose weekly paychecks bought American products and supported our economy.

The Japanese did not care about the conquered people. They looked at them as interlopers, people who were holding land and owning natural resources that should belong to Japanese businesses. The Japanese were imperialist. They wanted to move the locals out, conquered or not, and move Japanese settlers in. During World War I this meant immense profit for the Japanese.

As the Alaska Railroad was being built, it was a Golden Era for Japan. It was their moment of profit and the Japanese played international politics perfectly. By declaring war against Germany, a nation that could not defend its colonies, Japan had no opposition in seizing those German colonies. Japan also made money hand-over-fist by selling war material with no worry of being bombed by the Germans.

But Japan had a problem.

No matter what land Japan grabbed, it still had to feed all of its people. With the acquisition of more colonies, Japan needed more food. The Japanese preferred fish because of its abundance and low cost. This forced the Japanese to begin reaching further out into the North Pacific for fish. And there was Alaska, a land with lots of fish and very few soldiers. Two decades later, the Japanese would seize the last two islands of the Aleutians – Attu and Kiska – during the Second World War. Had the Second World

War turned out differently, Japan could have used Attu and Kiska as bases for long range aircraft to control the North Pacific. But today those islands are not necessary: the Japanese as businesses dominate the salmon industry.

But this is only a portion of the story affecting the long game for the Alaska Railroad. Domestically, the heyday of the construction of the Alaska Railroad took place in the most violent era of American history. It was an era of widespread bombing along with political and labor unrest. The era began in 1910 when the anti-union *Los Angeles Times* was bombed. On the night of October 1st, a union activist put a suitcase full of dynamite in the back alley of the *Los Angeles Times* next to some barrels of flammable printer ink. The dynamite was detonated with a cheap alarm clock. The initial explosion was aided in its destructive power with the rupturing of the natural gas pipelines in the building. Twenty-one people died in the explosion.

Six years later, two other bombs rocked the country. On July 22, 1916, 10 people in the Preparedness Parade in San Francisco were killed in a bombing, and eight days later, on the East Coast, the largest bombing in American history occurred. On July 30th, two million pounds of ammunition destined for the war in Europe on Black Tom Island in New York Harbor were detonated. The concussion was felt as far away as Maryland.

The decade of violence ended 60 seconds after noon on September 16, 1920, when a bomb was detonated on Wall Street. Forty people were killed and 143 were seriously injured.

For those who are interested in historical trivia, had the Wall Street bombing detonated seconds later it would have killed Joseph P. Kennedy and there would never have been a John F. Kennedy, Robert Kennedy, or Ted Kennedy.

Summing up the era, across America, labor radicals dominated the conversation on job sites. Anarchists, socialists, Bolsheviks, and syndicalists were, quite literally, everywhere and no one knew when the next act of violence would occur. Vigilance was required but the fact of the matter for the Alaska Railroad was there were labor radicals, anarchists, socialists, Bolsheviks, and syndicalists on every job site. The long game was to complete the railroad, period.

Fast forward a century later and the saga of Alaska on the northern rim of the Pacific Ocean has a new chapter. With global warming, the traditional ice-choked waters of the Bering Sea are relatively ice-free significantly longer. This has opened the possibility of the Bering Sea and Arctic Ocean to become the fabled Northwest Passage, the maritime waterway between the Pacific and Atlantic. The Russians recognize the profit potential and are advancing – militarily and, oddly, capitalistically, to seize control of the Arctic shorelines of the waterway. The United States and Canadian military are taking a hard look at the coastline on the other side of the opening Northwest Channel. The invasion of Ukraine by Russia has made every move, however slight, by Russia as cause for great concern. The total lack of concern for human life exhibited by the Russians in Ukraine is a chilling reminder of the action of the Japanese in their northward advance into the North Pacific.

Why did the Alaska Railroad last as a federal agency for so long?

If the Alaska Railroad was such an anomaly, why did it last so long? The answer is simple. There was no Plan B. That is, there was no highway that linked Seward and Anchorage with Fairbanks until 1971. That was half a century after the Alaska Railroad was completed. Until 1971, if you lived in Fairbanks, you had to get your heavy goods by cargo barge **once** during the summer, by truck from the Lower 48 through Canada, by air, or the Alaska Railroad. The Parks Highway – named for former Governor George Parks, not the Denali National Park – did not exist until community activist Mary Cary 'declared war against Governor Egan' to get the highway to link Anchorage and Fairbanks. Cary went on the manage Egan's winning campaign and then to work to have the highway completed.

Things in Alaska sometimes happen s-l-o-w-l-y. In retrospect, keep in mind the Alaska-Canada Highway, the roadway link between the Lower 48 and Alaska was not completed until 1942, two decades *after* the completion of the Alaska Railroad. Giving credit where credit is due, it is important to note the 1,600 miles of the Alaska-Canada Highway was also managed by the Army and one-third of the workforce were black troops.

TABLE OF CONTENTS

This book does not have a table of contents for a specific reason. The saga of the Alaska Railroad is not linear. That is, to understand the complexity of the construction of the Alaska Railroad and the backdrop of American history during the decade of construction, the reader must 'get into the weeds.' When you are 'in the weeds,' there is no clear picture of what is happening and when. Everything the workers knew, heard, understood and/or believed were simply pieces of a massive, real life, jigsaw puzzle. In real life, you will never see the 'whole picture,' so you have to arrange the tidbits of information, rumor and memo you have together for the best possible understanding of the matter. For you. But this is not necessarily the same for everyone else on the rail line.

Overall, this a book of ground level history of both the United States and the Alaska Railroad for the decade of the 1910s. It is history disguised as literature, a collection of personal snapshots, histories, memories and guesses of the day-to-day living and drama along with the nuts-and-bolts of the most unusual railroad in American history.

Enjoy.

Rat River

It was no secret why the Rat River was named.

It was named for a rat.

No surprise there.

But it was just one rat, a solitary rodent, not a passel. Actually, rats come in mischiefs. That's what the editor of the *Rat River Journal* told his readers. Not that anyone cared. The *Rat River Journal* was a kind of/sort of newspaper which came off the portable press once every once in a while when the editor, Hinton George, was sober.

Which was rarely.

Interestingly, as Hinton George wrote in the irregular *Rat River Journal*, while the namesake rat was a master of mischief, there was still only one. Where the rat had come from no one knew. How it survived everyone knew. It simply poached everyone's beans, fatback, bacon and salt pork. It scampered from cabin to cabin, entering through some crack in the log walls or up through the floorboards salvaged from sunken – or sinking – steamships on the tributary of the Yukon River. Once inside, the rat scurried about eating what it wished. Cats were no defense against the rat. Shrews, yes. The cats did a marvelous job of keeping cabins shrew-free. But the rat was another matter altogether. It was large. It was fast and it was fat.

But there was still just one rat; not a mischief.

Oliver Harrison was from New York, and he assured everyone – those who would listen – that the rat was, indeed, a rat. Being from New York, he knew a rat when he saw it. Both human and rodent.

The best guess was it had abandoned a steamer. Or scampered ashore from a steamer which had gone aground. Or sunk. Every oxbow of every tributary of the Yukon River had its share of derelict vessels, some beached but most deteriorating in the mud five or six fathoms down. The Yukon and Kuskokwim rivers supplied every Alaska Gold Rush boomtown from St. Mary's on the Bering Sea shore as far inland as Canada and the Arctic.

It was also possible the rat had been abandoned ashore by Russian fur traders. The Russians were famous rat people. This is not to say there was a biological link between the two, rather, it was a culinary one. The Russians plowed all the waterways and saltwater coastline of Alaska looking for furs. Not gold, just furs. To make sure their shipwreck survivors had something to eat, the Russians populated the shorelines of Alaska's rivers and the islands of the Aleutian Islands with rats. Then, if a Russian ship went aground – or under water – the survivors would have something to eat. Meat as opposed to edible vegetation of which Alaska had in sparse supply.

It was a fine theory but, frankly, if the rat had been a deposit of the Russians, the beast should have come ashore in a pair. It made no sense to drop a single rat anywhere. It would just live until, well, it died and that would be the end of the food supply.

But here it was, season after season, in Hadley's Mill.

Which was odd.

Twice, odd.

First, there was the rat.

Second, Hadley's Mill had no mill. It had a Hadley, George, and he was the reason there was a town. Actually, it wasn't a town, it was more of a settlement. Not even a village because it had no church, children or charity. It was just a dozen structures, two of them saloons. There was something equivalent to a General Store, brothel (of course) and a dilapidated barn. There were cabins in the vicinity, occupied or abandoned depending on the time of year and strength of the diggings on the three streams which fed the tributary of the Yukon River.

Hadley's Mill had not been named for a mill of the traditional sense of the term but, rather, a fish wheel. Most argonauts had never seen a fish wheel and when the first steamer had powered up the Rat River – yet to be named – someone had said the operating fish wheel 'looked like the waterpower wheel of a mill' and since Hadley sold the logs to the steamships when they anchored in the shoreline eddy, Hadley's Mill was christened.

The name became colloquially accepted when it was inked into the notes of the Yukon River steamer captains. It was not on the official, published map of the Yukon River because such did not exist. Thus the Rat River came to life in the myriad of hand-written logbooks of the steamer captains who spent the summer on the Yukon River and its tributaries from St. Mary's to Dawson. All 1,982 miles of the waterway – which did not include the 30-something waterway offshoots in both the Yukon Territory of Canada and the Territory of Alaska.

The 'big city' was Fairbanks, the penultimate destination of the steamships well up the Yukon River. Dawson had gone ghost so that left Fairbanks as the largest city on the river. More than 1,000 people called Fairbanks home. Or, at least, a domicile until they could strike it rich or go home broke. One did not live in Fairbanks; one wintered there.

But that was where the money was. It was odd but, then again, if you had spent time in cities in the lower states, money had many meanings. There was money that you earned and spent. When it was gone you had to make some more. Which you spent when you earned it.

But the money you spent had a life of its own. It passed from hand to hand, grocery to teamster to farmer or butcher or hatchery. Then the grocery store and teamster and farmer and butcher and hatchery paid their workers who spent the money in the grocery store for meat and eggs and potatoes and the teamster who brought the meat and eggs and potatoes to the store. It was a never-ending story. The money went around and around and around the city. In fact, that was what made a city: money moving around and around and around.

If you came from the lower states, called the "Lower 48" for the states that joined the union before 1921, Chena wasn't much of a 'big city.' But it was big compared to Hadley's Mill. What made Chena a 'big city' were the saloons. Rows of them, wall to wall, along both sides of the mud streets. They drew the argonauts like magnets attract filings. From a hundred miles away, up and down the Yukon and all its tributaries, the men were drawn to Chena for liquor, beans, liquor, women, liquor, pans, liquor and liquor.

Hadley's Mill was triple-blessed. First, it was situated on the edge of a deep-water eddy which made it a most excellent place for steamships to pull out of the powerful Yukon flow. Second, there were massive trees to the shoreline and from these timbers Hadley had made a lucrative living. He was a woodsman, and he spent all winter cutting down trees and reducing them to cords of wood, each log no longer than two feet in length and a foot in depth. These were the perfect dimensions for men to load onto the steamship and shove into the boiler below deck.

Hadley had found his gold in timber. It was just as hard as panning for the flakes in the rivers and streams and just as risky. Unless the steamship captains knew of Hadley's Mill, their ships would pass on by. Hadley's Mill, after all, was an eye-scratching town. If you were on watch and scratched your eye, you'd miss the town.

The third blessing was the waterfront trail. Winter and summer there was traffic along the footpath so there were always men willing to work in the logging business. Principally during the winter and particularly because Hadley paid in food and lodging in the abandoned cabins on his alleged-to-be property alongside the Yukon River eddy. These men were not skilled, knowledgeable or dependable but under the guidance of Hadley, the local hooch, beans and the ability to stay in an abandoned cabin during the winter at no cost, and they made Hadley a fortune. Then, come spring, the workforce would move along, searching for a stream, lake, or creek to pan for the elusive metal each man dreamed would make him wealthy.

Hadley's routine had been unbroken for a decade. When snow covered the ground, he and his crew of misfits would transform the forest into stacks of cords of timber. Come spring when the men moved on, up or down the Yukon, he would sell the wood to steamships coming up or going down the Yukon.

But Hadley's industry was dead. The beer and skittles were gone. The age of steam was over. The railroad was coming. Up from Seward, mile after mile, the Alaska Railroad was gnawing its way up the Interior. It would end in Fairbanks and overnight, the age of the steamship would be over. The Golden Age of Hadley's Mill was over. Everyone knew the end was near and they were packing to leave. The new nirvana was in Fairbanks. The new industry for unskilled workers was coal. Coal could be mined around Fairbanks and loaded into coal cars and shipped south to Seward. Wood was gone as an industry. And with the passing of the wood was the passing of Hadley's Mill. This was the last gasp of the steamship on the Yukon. When the vessels went down river this fall, they would be beached on the shore at St. Mary's. There they would be stripped by the locals for timbers, glass, metal and whatever else could be cannibalized for homes, saloons, and general stores. All that would be left would be the steel skeletons of the behemoths, rusting to oblivion.

And no one was thinking of the solitary rat. It was not going to be taken out of Hadley's Mill. It would simply remain in the ghost town, gnawing on what was left of the community. In the end, it, like Hadley's Mill, would pass into history, and, in the end, be only a footnote in a book of history.

At best.

LIEUTENANT OSCAR PENSACOLA

Editor
Nenana Telegraph
Nenana, Alaska

Dear Editor:

I take exception to your front-page story about the United States government stealing Alaska's coal. Being as informative as possible, let me give you three specific reasons you should consider doing a follow-up story that accurately reflects the reality of coal in the Territory of Alaska.

First, the coal fields in the United States are the property of the United States Department of the Interior so one cannot 'steal' something one already owns.

Second, the front-page story suggests the United States government is locking up the coal and Alaskans are being cheated of that resource. This is exactly the opposite of what is actually happening. While the United States government may own the coal, it does not harvest it. That is being done on contract to Alaskan companies. The United States Department of the Interior is hiring Alaskans to mine the coal, place the coal in rail cars, operate the Alaska Railroad to get the coal to the ports in Anchorage and Seward and load the coal onto cargo ships. Every penny paid to every Alaskan who participates in this work is spent in the Territory of Alaska. While the United States Department of the Interior may own the coal, it is paying a lot of pennies for that resource to transfer it from the ground to cargo vessels.

Third, the reason there is an Alaska Railroad is to move coal. In terms of investment, there are not enough people in the entire Territory of Alaska to make the Alaska Railroad profitable. What makes the railroad profitable is the coal. Alaskan coal is powering naval vessels all over the Pacific Ocean. This is a particularly important point for Alaskans to keep in mind. Currently, we have American forces in Siberia keeping the Bolshevik Russian government from overrunning Alaska. But Siberia is a long way from the West Coast of the United States. Everything our army in Siberia needs has to come by ship. Those ships are powered by coal. Today, and well into the next century, Alaskan coal will mean the difference between Alaska being part of the United States and being snapped up by some other country.

It is easy to say the coal in Alaska is Alaskan. It is. But coal has no value in the ground. It only has value when it is used. The United States Navy uses every ounce of coal mined along the route of the Alaska Railroad. The United States government is paying for every worker who has any part in the transfer of coal from the ground to the cargo ships. Focusing only on who owns the coal is a disservice to the reality of what is actually happening.

Hopefully, you will consider a news story that accurately shows how Alaskans are profiting mightily from coal owned by the United States Department of the Interior.

Sincerely,

BACKHAUL CHARLIE

It's the backhaul, son. It's all about the backhaul. The newspapers and folks on the street can say anything they want about the jobs and cargo being cheaper by the pound than with the auto-mow-beels but it's the backhaul that makes the difference. That's what makes a railroad profitable. Front end's up the rail with all the goods but if you don' have no backhaul then that incoming cargo is ex-pen-sive! Fairbanks got a lot of potential. Which is why we're here. None of that 'yes sir,' 'no sir,' up here. Down in Portland we were stuck. Could not move up because all the good jobs were taken. If you did not have a connection, well, you were stuck where you were. And we, your mother and I, did not like where we were stuck. So we came north. Fairbanks was wide open. Still is. Got lots of work for thems willing to work. We don't have a problem working. Summer and winter.

Here's why we're here. An' I don' mean Fairbanks. I mean right here on the flatlands. These ain' much now but we are gonna make it big here. See, the railroad is more than just a pair of iron rails runnin' through the wilderness. It takes an army of people to keep it runnin'. We're here at the right place at the right time. See, everyone on the streets is talking about how cheap goods are going to be coming up the railroad. They should. Right now we cannot get goods for 12 months every year. With the railroad we don't have to worry about the Yukon and Chena being frozen in. We don't have to wait for the steamship to come puffin' up the river. Seward is ice-free year-round. Yeah, there will be snow, deep snow, on the passes but, son, those locomotives got snow plows on the front.

So, here's what we're gonna do. Right now. We're going to get ahead of the game. We're gonna head out and homestead land that's got lots of trees. Tall ones. We're going to be lumbermen. The railroad's gonna buy timber for the cross ties and bridge foundation and buildings. If the railroad won't buy the trees, we can sell them to the folks here. Everyone's got to live somewheres and that somewheres is sure as shootin' going to come from wood, the kind of wood we'll be cutting down and milling. Even better, the Army's building the railroad. And the Army is gonna run the railroad. Those boys are going to have to live somewheres. They are going to need wood for the barrack and mess halls and meeting buildings. They'll come to us for the wood. We're gonna be millionaires, son. We're in the right place at the right time.

HAROLD MORGAN, ALASKA NORTHERN SCALPER

D arling! I told you it was worth every dime. But, no, no, you said buying shares in a dog like Alaska Northern Railway was a fool's bargain. Even at, what?, ten cents on the dollar. It was a hot item once. $3,616,800.81. I have no idea where that $.81 cents came from but, hey!, that was what the Interstate Commerce Commission reported as the total investment.

But that was eons ago in Stock Market time. Money is not a thing, Jeanine. It's ink on paper. Something to keep the new Internal Revenue Service from getting a dime. Overprice in on paper and then take a loss on paper somewhere else. As long as the ink at the end of the day is red, all is well. There's a lot of hiding of assets in that red ink. Lots of assets.

What? Where's our money? Darling! We bought in at ten cents on the dollar. Now the United States Government, thank you very much President William Howard Taft!, has ordered the Alaska Railroad Commission to buy the Alaska Northern for $1,157,339.49 – and I do not know where that $.49 came from, no! But yes, the United States government is going to buy our stock. That's what the Alaska Railroad Commission figured the railway was worth, about $16,000 per mile.

A lot of us Wall Street mystics – yes, I know that's what you call us – mystics, yes, yes, a lot of us Wall Street mystics are going to clean up. We are going to make an 800% return on our investment. And you know what is even funnier? We never spent an actual dime. That's right! Everything was on paper. Just ink on paper. A promise, that's all it was. Well, not actually no money. We did have to set up a front but all that cost was the lawyer. And he didn't cost. He took his fee in stock so I guess you could say we made eight dollars for every dollar we put in – and we didn't put any money in!

AIN'T AMERICAN CAPITALISM SPECIAL?"

HARRISON ANDERSON, HOMESTEADER

I don't think so. I mean. I'm following the law. Why don't you? This here land is mine. I filed it all legal and proper in Seward. The Homestead Act of 1862 provides that any adult American or adult who says he intends to become a citizen can claim up to 160 acres of survey government land for a homestead. As long as I did not take up arms against the United States of America – which I did not. I surveyed this land, all 160 acres of it, and I filed it all legal and proper in Seward.

What's that? Yes, that's true. The 160 acres next to me, in the path of where you want the railroad to be routed, is indeed owned by my brother. No. Just because he is in Pittsburgh does not mean he does not have Homestead rights. I have his signature on paper to file for him and I did. Yes, it is a pencil claim but it is leg-it-i-mate. And my cousin's homestead beyond that is leg-it-i-mate too. We all filed before you chose the railroad route so you cannot say we obstructed anything. And you cannot move us because we have a right to be here and until we do not improve the land in five years, it's our land.

Now, as a matter of principle, we, my brother and cousin and I, are not unfeeling individuals. But we have put a lot of effort into our lands as required by federal law. So, if the railroad really wants our property – which we are legally acquiring – it can make a reasonable offer. Or, yes you are right, you can take us to court under eminent domain but, you know, with lawyers, you could be in court until the day of Resurrection. Time's a-wastin' but it's up to you to make the first move."

JOSEPHUS AND PAYNE

The arrival of John Barton Payne along the rail lines in July of 1920, well ahead of any actual date of completion of the railway was no surprise to most of the workers. By 1920, the war in Europe was over and many of the men who had worked on the railroad before the war were not returning. Those men, who had been on the front lines, were used to visiting top-tier officers. These officers did not stay long but they did come.

But those top-tier officers were rarely generals. Generals were notoriously absent from the actual bloodshed. The higher your rank, the further from the front lines you were. Massive construction projects like the Alaska Railroad were different. There were front lines, per se, but there was no shooting. There were trenches but they were being filled with cement and the hubbub of battle was cursing of mosquitoes, the explosion of dynamite to remove geomorphic obstructions and the grumbling of the quality of foodstuffs on rickety plank tables along every running mile of line.

One of the blessings of work on the Alaska Railroad was the absence of the rain of artillery shelling. If you worked on the line – anywhere along the line – you were assured of the three important things in life: wages, water and longevity. But you still had to deal with the muckety mucks and, for most men, this was simply a matter of keeping your head low when they arrived, bow-and-scrap as required when such were in the vicinity and answered no questions.

The arrival of John Barton Payne was expected. After all, he was the second-highest muckety muck there was. The only one above him was the President of the United States, Warren G. Harding, and Presidents only showed up to cut ribbons. John Barton Payne was the United States Secretary of the Interior. He was the one who signed the checks for the Alaska Railroad – men, timber, cement, steel, food, ships, and fuel. You never messed with the man who signed the checks. They arrived, shook hands, made speeches and vanished. All you had to do when they arrived was the usual: keep your head low, bow-and-scrap as required and answer no questions. It was duck soup. As long as you weren't a simp, all would be well. The muckety muck would arrive, kick a few timbers, make some statements that have no substance and be gone.

But the shocker was not the arrival of United States Secretary of the Interior John Barton Payne. It was who came with him: Josephus Daniels! Daniels was the United States Secretary of the Navy and here he was overlooking the construction of the bridge over Hurricane Gulch, 200 hundred miles north of Seward. Yes, he traveled most of the way on the rail line but he was wearing shined shoes – **shined?! Shoes?!** Why? That was such a good question not a lot of people had an answer.

"MALAMUTE MIKE" DENSLOW, DREDGE OPERATOR

Willie, I am not the political type. I vote, yeah, but I vote for who I think is the best person for the job. Not party loyalty. Or politics either. I've voted Republican and I've voted Democratic. Was once an IWW man and I like the Progressives. I am not a Socialist because they are too closely tied to Russia and Europe where things have never been good for the workingman.

But, Willie, you are an avowed anarchist and, frankly, I think you are running down a very dangerous road. You're young and just starting in life and you look at what's going on in politics and business and life in general and see there is a lot wrong with the world. Has always been, sorry to say. Will always be. Life is not fair. It is not supposed to be. But there is not a dime of advantage in violence.

No, no, no. Just give me a few minutes to let you know what I think. I'm not your daddy, I'm your Dutch uncle, someone who ain' a relative but has good advice. First, violence, as in blowing things up, achieves nothing. If you have a problem with a business, you talk it out. If you blow things up, all work stops. No one gets paid. The bosses are the rich ones. They can just take their money and go. If that happens, all you've done is put a lot of working people out of a job. You don't hurt businesses by planting bombs, you ruin the lives of working people.

Second, when I was in the IWW, we talked a lot about the hydra. That was a Greek story you probably never heard. The way the story went, there is this monster with lots of heads. The Greek hero, Hercules if I remember from my schooling, was assigned to kill the hydra. But every time he cut off one of the heads another grew in its place. So he achieved nothing. The myth goes on, and it is a myth, that after Hercules cut off the main head, the hydra died. The point of the story was that in evil there is only one source and when you eliminate that source, all is well.

That ain' the way it happens.

I'll use an anarchist example.

One of the heroes of your brethren is Alexander Berkman. Right, the man who just got shipped to Russia. Back in about 1892, he was going to solve a labor dispute by killing the head of the hydra. In one fell swoop he was going to stop the strike, force the company to give the workers what they wanted and maybe even start the inevitable war between the workers and the employers. You know, replace capitalism with socialism. He used violence. What did it get him? Twenty years in the slammer. Did it stop the strike? No. Did it get the workers what they wanted? No. Did it lead to a change in how American business operates? No. It did squat. Nothing happened because violence will get you nothing but destruction of the means of making a living.

Now, for a better example, I operate a dredge. And I say I operate it because I do not own the dredge. The bank does. I am buying it from the bank. I have to pay the bank from the gold I get out of the bottom of the river. I can only pay my workers and the bank if I get gold out of the bottom of the river. Yes, I am a businessman. But I am a hostage of the economy. The price of gold is stable so to make more money, I have to find more gold.

I cannot find more gold unless the nuggets come up from the bottom of the river on the bucket line and my employees pull the nuggets out of the sluice boxes. What I pay my employees depends on the gold that comes out of those sluice boxes. If there is no gold, I have nothing to pay employees. But I still have to pay the bank even if there is no gold coming up the bucket line.

If an anarchist throws a bomb into my dredge, I'm out of business. My employees are out of their jobs. The bank does not get my payments which means someone else is not going to get a loan to start a business here in Fairbanks. Violence gets you nothing but rubble. There is no profit in rubble. There is no employment in rubble. And there is no future in rubble.

In a nutshell, Willie, the anarchists are not really American. They are terrorists. They believe if they destroy things, it will make America better. This is not true. And it is not American. Whether you like it or not, when it comes to business you can sum up America in a single statement: Can you cut a deal?

That's as American as you can get. In Europe there are all these kings and dukes and barons and whatever and they don't have to cut a deal. They've got lots of money and lots of land and they don't have to cut a deal with their workers. And they got that money and land a long time ago. That's not what's going on in America. Even with the rich folks. The business owners are rich because of the workers. Yes, because of the workers. But there are no royal families in America. The family businesses that made large amounts of dollars a generation ago are gone.

You want an Alaskan example?

OK, for the past 20 years the big money in Alaska has been with the steamships. They loaded up with the things Alaskans needed and then, over the summer, they powered up the Yukon and Kuskokwim rivers and sold those supplies for more than they cost in Seattle or Portland. They took gold onboard and went back down the rivers and got out of the Bering Sea before it froze over in September. They made a whale of a lot of money between June when the Bering Sea ice mantle broke and September when the ice froze over again. And they had been making those dollars big time for twenty years. But it's all over. The railroad is coming. When the railroad tracks reach us here in Fairbanks, we'll be getting supplies, tons of them, 12 months a year. We won't have to pull in our belts until the first steamships of the season arrive. Now, if you are not here by September 15, what you want is not going to come until June. Dogsleds and airplanes carry stuff by the pound. The railroad will carry it by the ton.

What's the example?

The steamships are gone. There is no longer a profit in getting cargo in Seattle or Portland or San Francisco and bringing those supplies up the river. That traffic is gone. The money is gone. What will happen now is some steamships will winter here in Fairbanks. Come spring they will load up with the tons and tons of cargo brought up from Seward by the railroad. Then they will take those supplies to the small boomtown and villages that are not on the railway line. But they are not going to be paying big bucks for those supplies. And the transportation costs will be small because the supplies are coming from Fairbanks, not Seattle or Portland or San Francisco. The big money in steamships is gone. Technology killed it. Terrorism had nothing to do with it. It's all economics, not bombs.

Willie, the future is not in violence. It is riding the inventions. It is taking advantage of the way things are right now. It's in cutting a deal. There is not a dime in blowing things up and putting people out of work. Keep that in mind next time you are in one of those monthly meetings with the socialists and syndicalists."

JOHNATHAN ALBERT,
TRACK LABOR SUPERVISOR

Now I know what all of you are thinking, and I agree with you. But there is nothing we can do about it. It's biology. The Spanish Flu is knocking the bejeezus out of our schedule.

Yes, the Governor has done the best he can but no one, and I mean no one, could have anticipated what happened. I mean, even if we had a vaccine, we could not have stopped the spread of that disease. The Governor tried. He tried to stop people with the Flu from coming ashore. But you don't have to be a Dumb Dora to know that was not going to work. I mean, one person with the Flu coming through and it's all over the Territory in the blink of an eye. Even the blockade of the trails didn't do squat.

Then things got very bad very fast.

So far it's been a vain effort because if one person with Flu slips through a quarantine, the quarantine is worthless. Someone did – apparently did – because a month after the quarantine the virus was ashore. When Governor Riggs ordered a *cordon sanitaire* on all trails leading to the Interior, that failed as well. It was speculated that the couriers who raised the alarm of the virus themselves were the carriers. And when Riggs requested federal help, $10,000 was allocated by the Senate and rejected by the House.

We were able to 'dodge the bullet' of the first wave of the disease but were not so lucky when the second wave hit in October of this year, 1918. Since the Territory has seen little impact from the initial strain, all of us became complacent. The *Anchorage Daily News* noted on October 21, 'Old Jack Frost sure put the crimp into Spanish influenza that is raging in the states and Anchorage is immune.' Eight days later, the *News* announced: 'Don't be alarmed over influenza in Anchorage; there is none and what seems so is just ordinary, common everyday grippe.'

But the *Anchorage Daily News* was in error.

Big time.

The oncoming waves of the Spanish Flu have been devastating the people of Seward and Anchorage and Fairbanks and even here on the line. The death rate is way up there. We're losing men right and left. Half the white population of Nome and more than half of the Inupiat in the region are dying. Across the Interior, the death rate is emptying the villages. To fight the pandemic, Governor Riggs has ordered people to stay in their homes and avoid public gatherings. This is not going to work. Particularly in the bush. Close contact with one's neighbors is, if not daily, then hourly.

Masks are being required in many communities but this has done little to stop the spread of the virus. Right now, hundreds of children are being left as orphans. In the bush, adults are so sick they cannot keep fires in homes burning so children and older people are freezing to death and there were reports of sled dogs eating human corpses because there is no one to feed them. So many white males are dying the Alaska Railroad has to hire Natives to work on the laying of the track.

The reason I'm telling you this is because some of you are going to Fairbanks for a break. You'd better be sure to wear your mask all the time. The Red Cross has hired a dozen men to walk the streets as healthcare deputies. If you look sick, they'll drag you to a hospital bed. And if you aren't wearing a mask, they'll bop you on the head and force you to put one on."

John Rutherford,
Alaska Railroad
Property Route Manager

Well, I'm sorry you feel that way, Chief. You are the Chief, right? This happened way above my head, Chief. Way up there. In Washington D. C. Technically, and legally I would imagine, Alaska was owned by the Russians. I don't know the details of the acquisition of Alaska from the Russians, but we bought it from the Russians in 1867, half a century ago.

Yeah, a while ago. You are right. And no, I do not know what arrangements the Russians had with the Indians. You are an Indian, right? Oh, OK, let's call them, you, Natives. All of you. Any arrangement you had with Russia went out the door when we, the United States, bought Alaska from the Russians. I suppose you could get some satisfaction, er, money, from the Russians but they ceased to exist about three years ago. There was a revolution and the Czar was given the boot. Killed, if I remember correctly. So there isn't even a Russian government you can sue.

As far as the United States is concerned, we, the federal government, own all of Alaska. There are no Native lands in Alaska the way there are in the lower states, like reservations, but individual Natives have the same rights as whites when it comes to homesteads. That's from the Alaska Native Allotment Act and Natives, again, individually, are protected from having non-Natives acquire their land.

Yes, 'steal' is a good word to use but only here in this office. Non-Natives cannot steal Native land without the consent of the federal government. That's under the *Berrigan* decision. Now, over the years, the General Education Agent for Education in Alaska, Sheldon Jackson, set aside quite a few reserves, as in land reserves, for the benefit of Natives. Some were small, say an acre, for a Native school while others were rather substantial, like hunting and fishing areas. But, as in all things having to do with the federal government, there were – and are – problems. Keeping this as simple as possible, land is money and when it comes to money, Congress has the legal power to spend it. Not the President of the United States. And it was the President of the United States, the head of the Executive Branch of the United States, who allowed the set-asides by Sheldon Jackson.

As far as what you are asking about, Native lands owned by all Natives that are in the path of the construction of the Alaska Railroad – we call that the transportation corridor – all I can say is Alaska is a Territory and now whatever a Native group says it owns has to be negotiated with Washington D. C. For Natives this will have to be done through the Bureau of Indian Affairs in the Department of the Interior. The Bureau is responsible for Indian rights and properties.

Actually, there may be a bit of luck for you here. Alaska is not a State yet so the Governor is actually an employee of the United States Department of the Interior. At this moment the Governor of Alaska, Thomas Riggs, Jr., has in-depth experience with Alaska – and the Alaska Railroad. He is the one who is responsible for the oversight of the construction of the railroad. He's the man you want to see about Native land in the collective. And he's in Juneau. I suggest you talk to him about Native land."

JERRY SANDUSKY, RAILROAD SPIKER

August 14, 1919
Mom,

Yes, I know it has been a long time since I wrote you last. I really did not have that much new to say. The work on the line is brutal. It really doesn't matter if it's summer or winter, each has its hardships. The Interior of Alaska, that's what it's called where we are working, does not have seasons like you do in Vermont. We only have two seasons here, summer and winter. And the change comes quickly. There are no fall colors here. Spring is just when the snow melts and floods everything. It's not really called spring. It's called breakup. That's when the ice that stretches across the river breaks up and moves downstream. Freeze-up is the opposite. It's when the surface of the rivers freezes from shore to shore. There is an old joke here that the Alaskan calendar only has three months and they all start with the letter 'J.'

The reason I have the time to write you is because I have the Spanish Flu. It is not pleasant, let me tell you, and I have to stay away from people for a while. So here I am, stuck in what we call a 'traveling cabin.' As the rail line is being built, where the men sleep and eat travels along with them. It's not really a cabin. That is, it's not made of wood. I guess you could call it a tent. It has no floor. The top of the tent has birch bark or moss or sod. The doors have hinges of leather or bent nails. And, it's got mud for a floor and hay for a mattress. Not uptown. It's pretty miserable living, but I am making very good money – $3 a day!! plus room and board. There are a lot of people in the Territory and Vermont who are not working at all.

There has been an influx of men since the end of the war, which is the reason, I think, the Spanish Flu made it this far north. Half of me is sorry I did not go to war. Some of the stories are chilling. But the other half of me did not want to stand in a trench that was nothing more than a sewer for 18, or 19 months.

Overall, the work has been exhausting. But it does pay well. And we earn our pay. During the summer the mosquitoes are so thick we need to wear nets over our heads and faces. There are so many they turn our pants and shirts black with their bodies. During the winter, which is about eight months a year, it is bitterly cold. Being inside is a blessing for the warmth but the smell is something I will never forget. We don't have washing facilities and we sure don't swim when there's snow on the ground. The privies are the forest and inside the cabin all the smells of cooking and bodies and the mixes we use on the line combine to a stench that will stay with me for the rest of my life.

The Spanish Flu is odd because not everyone gets it. Some do and some don't. I did but the other men in the cabin did not. I was wearing a mask, had to, and others were wearing masks. But I got the disease. Makes it hard to breathe. The other men, black, white, Japanese, Native and Irish, didn't get the disease. Why me? I don't know. No vaccine for the Flu so I'm stuck here waiting for it to pass. By the time you get this letter, I'll be back on the job. Wearing a mask, of course.

As long as I'm making the good money, I'll be here in Alaska. Cost of living is high but I'm making Alaskan wages so the cost of things does not matter. To me. That means more money when I come home.

Love!

Alaska Railroad Lobbyist Roberto "Bobby" Sandusky

Senator, I'm not here to tell you how to do your job. Being a Territorial Legislator is one tough job. Everyone wants something for free. And in the case of the Territory, you can pass all the bills you want on taxing the fishing industry and, frankly, both you and I know, the fishing industry is not going to pay a penny. If they do, it will be after a long court fight and at the end of the day there will be an out-of-court settlement of a dime on the dollar. If that.

But I am here today to suggest three things. First, you do not represent the area of the Territory that will be affected by the railroad. None of the dollars spent on the railroad are going directly into the pockets of your voters. But that does not mean your voters are going to be untouched by the railroad. In terms of actual dollars, everyone associated with the shipping industry is going to see a substantial change. Once the railroad is completed, your voters are going to see year-round shipping to Seward. Right now, all of the shipping to Fairbanks and up the Yukon and Kuskokwim rivers has been during the 120 days when the Bering Sea is ice-free. The steamships and barges with that traffic do not even stop in Southeast.

That is going to change. With the railroad, there will be a lot of shipping traffic bouncing up the coast to Seward. More ships mean more work for the voters in your district. And it means substantially lower transportation costs for cargo to your voters. Now they won't have to wait for a whole shipload to come north; the small items can come north on a Seward-bound cargo ship.

Second, you and the Territorial Legislature are looking in the wrong direction when it comes to the war. Yes, there is a war in Europe. But that's not the real danger here in the Territory. Alaska has everything an invading country would want: coal, gold, fish, fur, copper and oil. And Alaska does not have what every invading country fears: an army. If you add up all the men in any kind of a uniform in Alaska, we are talking maybe a thousand – and half of them are with the United States Coast Guard. Those men are not warriors, they are maritime marshals. Right now, as we are speaking, there are 7,000 United States Army soldiers in Siberia and 20,000 Japanese soldiers. The American soldiers are going to leave but the Japanese will not. They will be in Siberia for centuries. It will not be long before those Japanese look at Alaska and say to themselves, 'Why not take Alaska? Who's going to stop us? Look at all the money we could make with no one telling us boo.'"

Gerald O'Reilly, Cement man

Lieutenant, I've been in the concrete business since before you were born. There is no 'right way, wrong way, Army way' about it. It's what works. This is Alaska, not Kansas, and a lot of what you can do in Kansas will not work here.

A better example is the Panama Canal and I was in the Canal Zone. The ground in Panama – and here – is not stable. It is wet. We have pingos here and unless you have lived here for a while, you do not know what a pingo is. It's a frost heave. They come and they go. We have tundra here. It's solid in the winter and like a sponge during the summer. When we put down cement, we have to be careful because Alaska has ice down below. It's permanently frozen earth. As long as you don't mess with it, it is stable. The cement will not shift. If the cement does not shift, the foundation for the bridges will not shift. You don't have permanently frozen land in Kansas.

We've got a lot of mud in Alaska. That makes everything difficult. If you are not careful, the cross ties will sink. You won't know you have a problem until the tracks sink so low a train tips over. You don't have mud problems in Canada.

My advice. Listen to those of us who have been around the block since before you were born. We've seen the disasters of poor planning. There isn't a 'right way, wrong way, Army way.' There's the way that works."

CHARLIE BENSON, SOCIALIST

Charlie Benson, not a pseudonym, always found the third Thursday of every month an intellectual chore. And Benson was neither a scholar nor a teacher. He was an itinerant whatever. He had never made a profit at anything he had ever done. "Profit," of course, was a filthy word in his vocabulary. He wasn't a businessman; he was a worker. But he had to deal with business people to stay alive. Living had not been easy. He had worked on the railroad, in the mines, on the docks and even butchered chickens. He hadn't made much but everyone he had worked *for* had made thousands, maybe millions.

Benson was uneducated when it came to school books. But he was a master of survival. You had to be in these days. There was a war in Europe and it was sucking away every single penny in America. It was economics and Benson was a master at understanding the food chain of profit. Every company in America was selling to the European warlords. Both sides. In the open to the Allied Powers and through distributors to the bad people: Germany and Austria. Everyone knew what was going on. It was business, after all. That's what capitalism was all about: profit.

Which was why Benson was a socialist.

It wasn't something he was born to be or fell into courtesy of the clutches of a band of hoodlums. Rather, it had been a fast-arriving reality. You did not have to be schooled in Marx to know what was going on. All you had to do was keep your eyes open. You didn't even have to read the newspapers to see the truth. Businesses sold everything they could to the Allied Powers and the Central Powers. Which was why American businesses were running three shifts every 24 hours. It was all about profit. It wasn't who was doing the buying that was important; it was getting payment. Money had no nationality.

It also had no soul.

It was magical.

It would start as paper. Ink would be added and then the sheets would fly over ocean waters. When the paperwork landed in the United States it was swallowed whole and spit out as little sheets that swan-like migrating fish into banking nets from Bangor to Los Angeles. No one asked where the fish came from, just that they arrived.

Marx was correct when he wrote workers were being abused. Marx was right the workers of the world should unite. But Marx was wrong about it happening at all. Marx, after all, was an intellectual and those people never got blood on their hands or dirt beneath their fingernails. Marx certainly planted the seeds of revolution and tossed on the fertilizer, but he never lived to witness the plague of weeds he germinated which invaded the economic fields.

Benson had to do more than witness the pullulating of the weeds.

He had to live among them.

Every third Thursday of every month.

Odd it was, Benson thought, how poorly the so-called capitalists knew what was actually happening on the far side of their counter. Businessmen was actually a misnomer. There were no businessmen. Not in the United States, anyway. There were businesspeople in Europe. Or, were, before the war. Before the war, or so he had been told, the European businesses were small so every owner knew his employees. By name and occupation. Not so in America. In the United States no businessman ever ventured into the bowels of his own empire. There were minions between the owner and the worker. The minions were neither workers nor owners. They were employees and had no allegiance except to their paychecks. They were not workers and would not unite with either those above them on the business food chain or those below.

Benson was a socialist which, to the business owners high above and far away, was not just the tool of the Devil but Satan himself. To their mindset, socialists were the ones who wanted to own the businesses.

This was not wholly true but it was what the owners believed. The owners conflated – a word Benson used when speaking to other socialists – anarchists, socialists, syndicalists and union members into the same curse. The owners were fools and their distorted view of their own companies would one day pull them to ruin. Those who ran businesses lived in a world of apple pie and three-penny beer. They had apple pie and the workers lived on three-penny beer.

Benson was a socialist. He did not advocate violence, simply a change in the structure of the business world. To him, a business was not a profit-making entity. It was a service-providing operation. He was here in Fairbanks because the future of socialism was going to be born here. Here in Fairbanks. It was so simple he was surprised no one else could see it.

It was the railroad.

But it was far more than just a railroad. It was the future. A solid future. He had read the United States Constitution, the greatest document in the history of the world. It was biblical in the sense it charted the future from the past. Transportation was not included in the Constitution so roads and railways and steamship lines and even the air where planes were now flying were anyone's to exploit.

But there was a catch, a gift of the Alaskan gods.

Alaska was a Territory, not a state. And because it was not a state, it was not constrained by the same ink in the United States Constitution. One of the critical splashes of ink not in the United States Constitution was a railroad that was not in a state. Alaska was a Territory. So the land under the twin rails would be federal land. It would not have to be bought by a private company. And the railroad would be constructed with United States money. So there was no Wall Street investment involved. The Alaska Railroad would be operated by the United States government, not business people intent on squeezing every cent of possible profit. It was all United States government built, owned and operated. It was the perfect socialist tool. It was the future of labor come to earth. A golden opportunity to prove to the skeptical world that socialism was the future.

But there were problems.

And those problems reared their ugly heads every third Thursday of the month. Carrion in all forms draws buzzards, so too does money in any form draw vultures. The instant it was clear the Alaska Railroad had leaped from a Congressional pipedream to nuts-and-bolts reality, the hyenas magically appeared in droves. It was a mighty pie every shade of the radical universe wanted a piece of. The syndicalists wanted direct action immediately. They wanted to be in charge of all aspects of the railroad, from construction to cargo pricing, and threatened violence if they were excluded. The anarchists wanted to blow things up to show they were a force to be reckoned with. The pure Marxists were talking alliance with Russians even though there were no Russians in the Territory of Alaska and the Russian Revolution had produced nothing but the destruction of the working class. It was a boiling maelstrom of disparate views of unreality.

There was only one blessing to the gathering every third Thursday. The most ardent purveyors of violence in America had been exiled in December of 1919. A. Mitchel Palmer, the United States Attorney General, had ordered the round-up of the most virulent anarchists, socialists, and syndicalists and shipped them out of the country. All 249 of them were forced aboard the **USAT Buford** and exported to Finland. Then they were force-marched across the border into Russia. Thus the most vocal radicals were gone from American shores. This meant those radicals who were left had a sliver of decorum. Every sliver of that decorum was going to be needed here in Fairbanks because the Alaska Railroad was going to change not only America but the world. It was going to show the world that Marxism had legitimacy and the workers could own and operate what was, in every other part of America, a business.

But first, on every third Thursday of the month, Benson and his socialists had to keep the other revolutionaries from devouring their own in a political cannibal feast.

VLADIMIR IVANOVIC, BOLSHEVIK

Vladimir Ivanovic, real name unknown, took in Marxism with his mother's milk. She and her husband were Marxist converts long before Vladimir Ilyich Ulyanov became Vladimir Lenin. Bolshevism was the corrupt offspring of Marxism. It was also doomed to be a failure. True Marxists saw Bolshevism as simply the expected historical deviation from the basic precepts of world revolution.

And that was what estranged Vladimir Ivanovic from his kith and kin. They were intent on a world revolution of the working class. Vladimir saw the basic flaw in this fantasy. The working class was composed of followers, not leaders. The leaders of Marxism saw the masses for what they were: sheep. They could be led but there was no place to lead them. Worse, the so-called Workers of the World were a figment of economic theory. Not only did each city, province, nation and region have its idiosyncrasies, but so did every industry.

And every tier of those industries.

Into this bubbling cauldron of philosophical delusion was tossed the reality of nationalism. French coal miners were, after all, French and when the war started in 1914, French coal miners viewed German and Austrian coal miners as the enemy. The same was true in reverse. So, philosophically, while all coal miners were cut from the same bolt of Marxist cloth, that was no real-world reality. The split was made even wider when French coal was cheaper on the world market than German coal. This had nothing to do with the coal workers but everything to do with the cost of rail transportation. French coal fields were closer to the Atlantic shipping lanes than German or Austrian coal. So French coal was cheaper. Which infuriated German and Austrian coal miners. Along with German and Austrian coal mine owners.

This was not to say Marxism was a bust.

It was simply flawed.

Badly flawed.

It was a fine starting line for the race for cash for the working class. But it was an unworkable theory. To make it workable, three things had to happen in sequence. First, there had to be a government in place that would force industries to pay the workers in that country what they were owed. Second, the workers had to blindly agree to all decisions by the government. Third, individualism had to be eliminated. There could be no deviation from the mainstream.

These would never happen. So the next step was the inevitable, historical conclusion. There was too much money being sequestered by the upper class. This had to change.

But there was a problem.

In Russia, that is.

Anyone who had spent any time in Europe knew that Russia was a backwater. It had every economic feature working against making Russia a world power. First, it was so vast, transportation costs drove up the price of Russian products. Second, the Russian government spent very little money on civil improvements. The only notable exception was the ongoing construction of the Trans-Siberian railway which would bring fish and coal from the Pacific to western Russia. Third, Russian society was stuck in the Middle Ages. The rich had more than they needed and squandered it on products not made in Russia. So money was enriching the fashion houses and jewelry exchanges of Italy and France. As the rich made more money, more of that money was shipped out of Russia. Only a revolution would start a redistribution of wealth. And even if there were a revolution, it would still take several generations of Russians to catch up with the European economy.

If Russia ever could.

For dedicated revolutionaries, the United States was the promised land. Its economy was so large that massive amounts of money trickled down to the working class. Even more important, the upper class was fluid. There were no royal families. Those who became rich were those who became rich. When their heirs lost money, the families faded from view. Also, unlike Russia, there was always room at the top. There was not a set routine for becoming American royalty, you either had money or you did not. Those who had money were American royalty. If their children could not build on the family fortune, they disappeared from the upper ranks.

But the bottom-up problem in the United States was the same as in Russia. The working class was still locked in poverty. There was no mechanism to improve the income of the working class. It was the age of Social Darwinism and the businesses of America were locked into the social insanity of 'survival of the fittest.' Even on a biological level this was idiotic. The fittest fish were not the ones that survived. The surviving fish were the ones who found a food source and stayed with it. The larger the food source, the more fish. Survival was thus a matter of propinquity, not physical stamina. All mayflies will die so there are no 'fittest.'

And the mosquitoes which survive to breed the next generation are the ones who find warm-blooded prey who wander onto the minuscule acreage where some mosquitoes can fly – and only on days with no wind.

Moving up the food chain, the fittest human beings were not the ones who survived. It wasn't the richest either. Sometimes it is just luck. Take the trenches in Europe. Mortar shells fell where they fell; they did not discriminate between the 'fittest' of the enemy and 'weakest.' The survivors were not the fittest, just the luckiest. When a ship sinks, everyone goes under, the fittest along with everyone else.

Unlike other Bolsheviks and, for that matter, socialists and anarchists, he was no fool. This was because he was a student of history. A revolution, like the one raging in Russia at that moment, had – historically speaking – one of three outcomes. First, like too many revolutions in history, the revolutionary leaders would simply replace the upper class they had just eliminated. The same schemes, scams and subterfuge would erupt from the revolutionary soil but with different hands taking in the harvest.

The second outcome of the revolution was either immediate, out-and-out anarchy or a slow spiral into the deepest recess of chaos. The murder of Julius Caesar on the Ides of March in 44 B.C. led to a ten-year civil war which only ended in more bloodshed 13 years later. While 13 years is in the blink of any eye when one is reading ancient history, to the Roman citizens it was 13 seasons of famine, disease, and thousands of dead, many of whom had not supported any one of the contenders. The American Civil War only lasted four years but more than 650,000 were killed. And that did not include the injured, maimed, diseased, and infertile survivors – and there was no doubt the animosity of the South was going to fester for many generations to come.

Another example of a revolution doing nothing more than beginning a slow spiral to anarchy was the French Revolution.

The French Revolution was doomed to failure for a number of reasons. First, and most likely, the revolutionaries did not have the ability to keep the basic economics of the country going. The revolutionaries executed those wealthy French citizens who had not fled. This deprived the country of the knowledge of how to keep the country's economy going. The same thing happened with the Spanish Inquisition. The concept was to eliminate the non-Christians from Spain and, at the same time, taking their businesses. The general belief of Ferdinand and Isabelle and their court was that Christians could simply replace the Jewish business people. After all, if the winery or import/export business was profitable, it really did not matter who owned it. The problem was for a business to remain profitable, you had to know what you were doing. The Jewish wineries and import/export businesses had been successful because they had survived all of the mistakes the usurpers were going to make. So, the Spanish Inquisition went broke, and the era of Ferdinand and Isabella was the high watermark of Spanish culture.

The only thing that saved the French from following the same plunge to disaster was the rise of Napoleon. By the time Napoleon seized power, the French people were begging for economic stability. They were broke, hungry and fed up with successive, incompetent, petty, bickering, feuding of the revolutionary governments who were supposed to have brought peace and prosperity to France.

But the primary reason Ivanovic was in the United States and working on the railroad was because the Americans had shown the world you could have a revolution that did not end in disaster. Even more important – which gave his Bolshevik soul hope – was that America was a land where the workers could gain enough control to have a meaningful seat at the bargaining table. This had never happened in Russia and would never happen in Russia.

Spain was third-rate power and the Roman Empire was no more. But in the United States the workers were on the rise. A dozen years ago, a union was a pipedream. Today, it was a reality. Why, in the Spring of 1894, Eugene Debs had fomented a nationwide railroad strike. NATIONWIDE! Yes, it was not successful but the message across the United States was clear: an era of unionization was rising. But Debs had run for President of the United States twice since then. There were great changes coming to America.

The Alaska Railroad was the perfect place for Bolshevism. True, it was not traditional Bolshevism in the sense that the government was controlled by the workers. But it was a place where the workers were so important to the work of the railroad their demands could not be ignored. If the workers on the Alaska Railroad made demands for higher wages and other benefits, those demands would have to be met. The alternative was to wait for months for workers to come to Alaska from the Lower 48.

The time for an American brand of Bolshevism was nigh.

MITCHEL PALMER,
ATTORNEY GENERAL OF THE UNITED STATES

It is going to take well more than a century to judge the Attorney General of the United States, A. Mitchel Palmer. Even then, his legacy is still in dispute. Even more important – both in his time and well into the future – was the unanswered question as to the extent of the reach of the federal government and lack of restraining statutes, regulations, laws, traditions and common-sense end-around runs.

Until October 22, 1917, Palmer had a reputable record of public service. He represented a district in Pennsylvania in the United States House of Representatives from 1909 to 1915 and, as a Democrat, he aligned himself with the wing of the party that advocated significant social change. He was convinced to run for the United States Senate in 1914 but he was soundly defeated, coming in third.

He was out of public view when the First World War began and proved to be out of step with most Americans when he said of the sinking of the LUSITANIA that "the entire nation should not be asked to suffer" because the American passengers had taken passage on a ship that was carrying munitions to the war front. American businesses were in favor of the war because it meant huge profits and Americans in the street believed the war in Europe would eventually spread around the world. When the Russian Revolution occurred, there was great fear that the pestilence of Bolshevism would find root in the United States.

Considering the First World War occurred in the middle of the most violent decade of labor violence in American history, there was reason to be concerned.

Very concerned.

Even more important, as history would record, the violence would not abate until well into the next decade.

On April 6, 1917, President Woodrow Wilson formally declared war on Germany. Very quickly Congress passed three acts that altered the American landscape. Two of them were somewhat reasonable. The Espionage Act of June 15, 1917, outlawed the collection of any pictures or information with the intent to sell the gathered material to cause "injury to the United States." Shortly thereafter, on October 6, 1917, Congress passed the Trading with the Enemy Act which gave the President the power to restrict trade with Germany and its allies. Then came the bombshell, domestically speaking.

In the next year, on May 16, 1918, came the Sedition Act which shredded the First Amendment of the United States Constitution. Worse, the wording was so broad it invited abuse. Quoting from the Sedition Act itself, "disloyal, profane, scurrilous, or abusive language" was subject to arrest and imprisonment. Disloyal language was easy to ascertain. But "profane, scurrilous and abusive language" pretty much defined one-quarter of all language being spoken in the Territory of Alaska and seven-eighths of all language of the rail line crews.

With the hysteria of war in poisonous bloom, in 1917, by Executive Order, President Wilson established the Alien Property Custodian who was "empowered to receive all money and property in the United States due or belonging to an enemy, or ally of the enemy, which may be paid, conveyed, transferred" and who was "empowered to receive all money and property in the United States due or belonging to an enemy, or ally of the enemy." In the language of the streets of America, it meant if you were a German or Austrian your business and property could be legally snatched from your possession.

There was also another Constitutional wrinkle. In direct violation of the Fifth Amendment of the United States Constitution, the Alien Property Custodian could sell the seized property. And the money seized would not be given to the former owner of the property. There was no "just compensation" for the private property seized by the government.

If this was not un-American enough, there was yet *another* wrinkle. The Alien Property Custodian could sell the seized property and *keep* the money. This gave the Alien Property Custodian a power only delegated in the United States Constitution to Congress: the right to spend public money.

By 1918, Palmer as the Alien Property Custodian had accumulated seized over 300 property and amassed more than $500 million in assets – and anticipated seizing another 9,000 properties worth another $300 million. The properties seized included breweries, manufacturing operations, raw land and small business. With no one in the government overseeing the Alien Property Custodian, Palmer sold the assets as he wished or put friends and political allies in charge of the multimillion-dollar properties he had seized.

The seizure power of the Alien Property Custodian created a real problem at the street level. What was a German? Was it someone who had been born in Germany but had become an American citizen? Was it a German who was becoming an American citizen? How about an American with an Austrian wife? Or an Austrian man with a Canadian wife? Or a company that was partially owned by a German? How about the children of Germans or Austrians born in the United States? All of these legalistic twists and turns were particularly troubling to the Territory of Alaska because many of the mine workers, stampeders, fishery employees and men building the Alaska Railroad were of German and Austrian origin.

Then, Constitutionally speaking, the situation got worse.

In March of 1919, Palmer was confirmed as Attorney General of the United States. He began his tenure by releasing more than 1,000 Germans who were in federal custody. The war in Europe had finished in November of the previous year so there was no reason to continue to hold foreign nationals in detention camps. But it did not take long for a new enemy of democracy to emerge. In addition to race riots across the nation, there was a flurry of bombings, today called domestic terrorism. A turning point for the Attorney General came in April of 1919 when 36 dynamite-filled packages were sent to leading American newspaper editors, businessmen and judicial officials – including Palmer.

The bombing was the last straw for most Americans. There were radicals everywhere in the country and no way of tracking them much less stopping the bombing. So, Palmer resorted to eliminating the radicals altogether in one fell swoop. In November of 1919, the Justice Department teamed up with local police departments across the country and rounded up as many known radicals as they could find. These were known as the Palmer Raids and very little effort was made to protect the Constitutional rights of the arrested individuals. They were unceremoniously apprehended and, on December 21, 1919, the supposedly 249 worst, were placed on the **USAT BUFORD** in New York harbor and shipped to Russia. It was said this was "America's Christmas present to Lenin and Trotsky." Americans were ecstatic and believed the 'disease of anarchy and bombing' had been swept from American shores. "Just as the sailing of the Ark that Noah built was a pledge for the preservation of the human race, so the sailing of the Soviet Ark is a pledge for the preservation of America," the *New York Evening Journal* editorialized.

But there was more than one problem.

First, there was only one radical on board the **BUFORD** who had been convicted of a terrorist crime, Alexander Berkman. Second, the only radicals who were rounded up were the visible ones. The most violent anarchists were, to use a modern term, well under the radar. Proof of the failure of the Palmer Raids to get all of the violent radicals off the street became apparent the next year, on September 16, 1920, with the bombing of Wall Street in New York.

Third, there was a ripple effect across the country.

It did not take long for the impact of the war in Europe to reach the Territory of Alaska. During the course of the war, the Sedition Act was used to generate a host of legal cases which, under normal circumstances, would have been ignored by the authorities.

In March of 1917, John Schmidt in Haines was arrested and tried in the United States Commissioner's court in Haines for "defiling the Stars and Stripes." The jury found him Not Guilty "but before dismissing the action," Schmidt was required to "salute and kiss the flag, which he did."

In Eagle in August of 1917, Jean Albrecht, was arrested as she was entering the Territory of Alaska from Dawson. Albrecht, German by birth but Canadian by citizenship, spoke "English with a foreign accent. Her intense interest in the war while a resident of Juneau may have excited suspicion."

In Iditarod, Jack O'Neil was arrested for "using obscene language and for utterance against the President bordering on the treasonous." In fact, he called the President of the United States "a vile, unprintable name" and was alleged to have made "other rabid utterances."

Sometimes the laws were used as a cudgel. In 1918, two newspaper editors were charged with Draft violation and Sedition for publishing five comments which were actually true:

1. The sinking of the **LUSITANIA** was justified as she was carrying food and munitions to the Allies;
2. The execution of Edith Caville as a spy was justified;
3. That Lord Northcliffe, who controlled 16 large newspapers in the United States, "had stated" if England gave him enough money, he could "buy up public opinion enough in the United States to get the United States into the war;"
4. That England and France had a secret deal against Germany; and
5. That TR "had said that the Kaiser was the most wonderful man that Europe had ever produced."

Also in 1918, three individuals were charged with sedition because they had tried to slow down work at an Alaskan cannery for higher wages. Fish were "war material" so the three were charged with sedition for "wrongfully, unlawfully, willfully, and feloniously attempt[ing] to injure and destroy war material, to-wit, fish food." A similar incident happened in Loring and the individual involved was charged with sabotage.

And some of the cases were downright laughable.

But they were considered by the court to be worthy of prosecution. In 1918, the President and Secretary of the Alaska Labor Union were prosecuted for "discrimination against military uniforms" because they had refused to allow three men in uniform to attend a "smoker." [A "smoker" was a boxing event. It was not called a "boxing event" because "boxing" was illegal in the Territory.]

In July of 1918, James Brennan of Petersburg, berated two United States Navy officers in his brothel. The officers claimed to be secret agents even though they were dressed in uniforms. According to court documents, Brennan used "insulting language" and made a "slighting remark about the naval uniform." According to the legal file, the un-American statement made by Brennan was

> By-God I want to know what God Damned business you guys has got here anyway, tell me God Damn you I want to know, and I want to know what authority you have got for being here, I am going to see about this thing.

And in 1917, Bruce Brown was charged with "selling liquor to troops." This was an odd charge because, technically, the only 'legal' liquor in the Territory of Alaska was for medical uses. This, of course, was a crock and every community in the Territory had a blind pig. The only charge regarding the selling of liquor which resulted in convictions was the selling of liquor to Natives. Oddly as well was the charge Brown had sold liquor to troops "from his saloon" which could not be because there were no legal "saloons" in the Territory. The alleged illegal substance was presented as evidence in court and one witness identified it as "beer" while another stated that "it looked like beer but seemed flat." Brown claimed it was a "cereal beverage guaranteed to be free from alcohol." It came as no surprise that Brown was found "not guilty."

Occasionally the court did take the violation of Constitutional rights seriously. In February of 1919, three months *after* the war in Europe had been concluded, seven men in Ketchikan were tried for "Incitement to Riot." They had publicly seized three Norwegians who the seven defendants claimed were "slackers." [Seven decades later, "slacker" meant "draft dodger."]

The three Norwegians were draped with yellow ribbons and marched back and forth across Ketchikan with a placard reading "SLACKER" on their chest. The Norwegians were then taken to the edge of a Ketchikan pier and forced to jump into the water below. Pulled out of the bay, they were tied with ropes and dragged behind a car for several blocks.

The Alaska Railroad was not immune from the impact of the Sedition Act. According to seven witnesses in the tent where Ed Lund and members of an Alaska rail line crew were housed, Lund – on about Mile 237 – made seditious utterances against the government of the United States and the President of the United States.

It was reported and investigated Lund had stated to the men with whom he was living in an Alaska Railroad tent that he was, in his words "a German and at war with all American sympathizers." He also stated numerous times to the men in the tent that if any of his comments were reported to the United States Marshal, he would, again in his words as reported in court documents, "kill them all and scatter their brains on the logs." Lund was also accused of stating he wanted to get into the American Army so he could "turn around and shoot the officers."

Further, Lund made disparaging remarks about President Woodrow Wilson and asserted the President was a "d--- fool for bringing the [United] States into the war, and he hoped [the Americans] would get a good licking [and that] the President should be shot for [bringing the United States into the war.]"

At trial, Lund was a hostile defendant and persistently interrupted the proceedings, claiming the witnesses were liars and stating they did not know what they were talking about. Further, he asserted that his hard-drive workforce manner made him disliked by many men, some of them being in the contingent who had made the "erroneous statements" at his trial.

Lund claimed the men had put together a case against him with the material they, quoting Lund, "must have read that stuff in a magazine."

Lund was found guilty of sedition and sentenced to a year in prison.

HAROLD DUNCAN, GANDY DANCER

Jerry, I've been a gandy dancer for nigh on 50 years. 50 years! Started when I was 15. After the Civil War. I'm not *that* old! No, I did not work on the Pacific Railroad. That was the old name. I'm surprised you know that. Today it's called the Transcontinental Railroad. Before that, and after it was called the Pacific Railroad. Three different companies made that line. They're all gone now.

I was never up there in the management. I wanted to be, but it never happened so I'm still working at 65. This is going to be my last job. Swear it. I don't have a lot of money but enough. I can't live in Alaska because it's too expensive. And too cold. But too expensive is good. No, really! See, to get men to come up here, the Alaska Railroad has to pay more. That's good because our money goes right into the bank. In my case, three of them. I remember the Crash of 1892 when lots of banks went belly-up. All my money was in one bank and I was out of luck. I'm smarter now. Divide my money into three parts, one for each bank. That way if one goes bad, I've still got two banks in business. And I'm going to retire someplace hot. Too cold for too long up here.

Gandy dancer? Old term, yeah. When I started, the big manufacturer of tools, railroad tools, that is, was the Gandy Manufacturing Company. Out of Chicago. That's where I started working the rails. And we kind of danced around spiking in the rails or repairing them. That's where the term gandy dancer comes from. Not that many men are called gandy dancers anymore. The older ones, yeah. Young ones like you, just workers. Maybe even union men if the vote goes through.

A lot of terms of the old days are gone now. 'Highballing' meant you were good to go, and the engineers were called hogsheads because of the hats they wore. Not a lot of hump yards up here now. But you wait. When they get the spur lines in, yeah, then you will hear the term.

Let me give you some advice, Jerry. I made a lot of mistakes in my life. Ones you do not have to make. If you want to be successful, you have to do three things at the same time. First, you've got to read. Newspapers especially. You have to know what is happening. Then you can see where you fit in the big picture. Second, know your history. Things do not just happen. They happen for a reason. This railroad is a good example. No one is going to tell you why the railroad is here. Just that it is. But use some common sense.

What's that? An example for this railroad?

OK. Right now the population of Fairbanks, where this train-line is headed, might be 1,000 people. And Seward where the train started has about 500 people. Toss in Anchorage, and you have another, say, 800 people. That's not a lot of folks but the United States government is willing to spend more than a million dollars to build a railway. That's a lot of expense for very few people. So there has to be something else happening here. The federal government is not going to spend that kind of money for so few people.

Why?

Jerry, you've got to read your history. And you've got to be bright and smart. One ain't no good without the other. Being bright means you know a lot. But being bright does you no good unless you use what you know. I've known a lot of men who had college degrees but weren't smart enough to tie their own shoes.

So, for your education, Jerry, I'm going to give you some basics. You should read the history of railroads so you can see the future. First, with the exception of this one, all railroads are started and run by private companies. This one is being built and will be run by the government. That's good news and bad news. It's good news because no one has to worry about making a profit. People do all kinds of crazy things to make money. Things like cutting back on quality, packing too much cargo in too small a space, and letting repairs go longer than they should. When the government runs the rail line, there is an employee for every function. Those employees stay employed by keeping the track ship-shape, to use a sailing term. The road does not have to make a profit so there will not be any cutting back on the quality of service.

But having government run things is not necessarily a good thing. High-quality people can get better-paying jobs elsewhere so they leave. Over the long term, the people who stay are not the best. And since they do not have to make a profit, their job is secure. To get a retirement, all they have to do is put in 20 years. So, every day at work is just one day closer to retirement.

Now, here's where bright and smart come into play for this railroad. Even though this railroad is being constructed by the government, it still has to serve a purpose. So you look for that purpose. It does not take a Thomas A. Edison to figure out what's what. Just look at the reality of the railroad. When you study railroad you will find we are doing exactly what has to be done to produce a quality line. You need lots of cement and steel and spikes and cross ties and lots of men working and lots of money for pay and lots of food for meals. We've got all that. And you will notice that every mile of track that is laid there is a mile to telegraph wire alongside the track. We are doing very well when it comes to construction. That's the bright part.

Now comes the smart part. Here's where you can see the future, Jerry, and plan for the long term. For a train to be profitable – and this one has to be profitable in some way or the United States government would not be funding it – there has to be another purpose. So you look for that purpose by studying history. The history of railroads in the United States – and Europe too, I'm betting – is not the transportation of cargo. Yes, the train gets paid for transporting cargo from, say, a dock somewhere to a man who wants to buy that whatever. But the railroad has to make more money. That's what killed railroads in the South before the Civil War. The trains running south could carry lots of goods, but if there was not a backhaul, the boxcars came back empty. The big problem with getting a train to run to the South before the Civil War was that there was nothing to put in the boxcars. No, not cotton. Cotton was put on barges and the barges floated down to New Orleans where the cotton was sold. It did not cost the plantation owners anything to transport five tons of cotton to New Orleans when they used the rivers. But if the cotton was put in a boxcar, it was going to cost so much per pound. No one was willing to pay the railway to move cotton if the cotton could be floated downriver for free.

The point? Jerry, even though this railway is being constructed by the United States government, it still has to have a backhaul to be profitable. This railway was not built to get goods to Fairbanks. It was built to get something out of Fairbanks. That's the future of this railway, Jerry. What you have to do is figure out what the backhaul is and position yourself to be in the right place at the right time to take advantage of that backhaul. Be smarter than I ever was."

WILLIE THE WEASEL

"Jimmie, Jimmie, Jimmie. You just don't get it. Pull your head out of the mud. Or, I guess you could say, tundra. Matters not. Jimmie, don't you understand. We are not duping some guy or some business or some company. The Alaska Railroad is managed by the United States Army. It's not like robbing a bank. There's no one on patrol on the railway. Even better, we can double sell!

See, the way I figure it, there is no way the Alaska Railroad can keep track of all of its property. I mean, the rails and spikes and cross beams. An' no one is watching them rails and spikes and cross beams. They are just sittin' around. Yeah, there are some Army guys who are supposed to be watching the railyard but there are no cops or marshals.

So, here's what we do. We snatch some rails and spikes and cross beams and hid 'em in the woods. No one is going to go looking for anything in the forest. Then we sell the whole kit and caboodle back to the railroad. They are buying lots of stuff. We are not even small potatoes. Even better, we're not the only entren-whatevers they're called. We are just a different breed of businessman. Besides, like I said, ain' no cops or marshals on duty. We're talking the Army building the Alaska Railroad. No cops, no marshals, just a few of us making some good money reselling what we find in the forest. Got it?"

Josephine Carlos, Suffragette

Now Harriet, Alaska is not Kansas. Yes, I know, you are from Kansas. Everyone in Alaska is from somewhere else. Or their parents were. Heck, even the Alaska Natives are from somewhere else. We're all immigrants here. Refugees in many cases.

I'm thirty years older than you, Harriet, and I've been through a lot more scrapes in my life than you will ever be through. America's on the verge of a huge renovation. In ten years you will not recognize the America of today. I predict, and I can do that because I'm a codger, America is going to boom and bust at the same time. It's going to boom because every country in Europe is down to the bedrock destroyed. Europe is going to have to rebuild and the only people who can make that happen is us. We are not going to rebuild Europe but we are going to provide the cement and steel and brick and wire that will rebuild Europe. And all of that cement and steel and brick and wire is going to be provided by American companies who hire American workers and use American raw material. Labor is coming of age.

Second, Prohibition is going to be a complete failure. It's not even a good idea. Frankly, because I am in the management of the railroad, I have to live in two visual worlds. That is, officially, there is no alcohol on the Alaska Railroad. That's the federal law and the Territorial law and railroad policy. Unofficially, I know there is a problem with alcohol on every mile of the railway. In Seward and Fairbanks, you have to be blind not to know there are blind pigs – and I like that pun.

Third, which is the reason I'm talking to you, is you women are chasing the wrong rainbow. You put all this energy into getting the 19th Amendment passed and, frankly, it meant nothing. Women were already voting in Alaska, for instance, before the Amendment passed. So, basically, you got nothing. At least nothing new. Now, in some states where men still live in caves, so to speak, giving women the right to vote was a good thing. But there were – and are – bigger fish to fry.

Right now, Harriet, I have to pay you half of what a man would make for the same job. That's not right. The point of equality is to be treated equally. Right now, women are not. The way the Army dodges the issue on the railroad is to give women jobs that only women will get. That way there is no way for women to say they are being paid less than men for the same job. But the fact of the matter is they *are* being paid less than men.

By the time you get to my age – and I swear I am 35 – women are going to be tired of being treated like second-class citizens. But that is not going to happen until enough women get off their couches and out of the kitchen to demand equality. The reason I am telling you this is because I have three daughters and I do not want to see them working at the same job as men and getting paid half as much. I am giving you advice now so my daughters can get paid what they are worth, not less than the man working alongside them.

It's a simple fix, Harriet. Next time the equality of women comes up, don't come up with a new Amendment. Simply fix the old one. Move to amend the 14th Amendment and add the word 'sex' along with race, color, creed and previous conditions of servitude. It's a simple addition but don't wait for a century to get it done."

HORATIO SANDRONI,
ACCOUNTS RECEIVABLE

Nice of you three to meet with me. But then again, this meeting never happened. Men, have you ever read ALICE IN WONDERLAND? I didn't think so. Nothing personal now. You should read it. One of the greatest books ever written and if there is any one book everyone working on this rail line should read it's ALICE IN WONDERLAND. Why? Because we have fallen down a rabbit hole.

Let me explain. Basically, Alice, a normal child, follows a rabbit and falls down a rabbit hole. On the way down the rabbit hole, and in the fantasy world at the bottom of the rabbit hole, logic and reasonability do not matter. It is a whirlpool of fantasy and irrationality. The point I am making here is that you, all three of you, and me, live in a rational world. All of us have been on many construction projects over the years and, to use an old expression, we know what's what. But this Alaska Railroad has been a rabbit hole since the idea of a railroad popped up under President Theodore Roosevelt.

First, the original intent was to have the railroad built on the same management model as the Panama Canal. You know, let the Army do it. The Army did a good job in Panama building the canal so why not duplicate the success in Alaska? Whoever came up with that idea must have done it late at night in some tavern with too many empty bottles in front of him. The Panama Canal was a success because the workers were almost all blacks, Haitians and other nationals from the Caribbean who were used to being treated like serfs. Not slaves because they got paid. But serfs. Serfs do what they are told. They do not form unions; they do not backtalk supervisors; they eat what is served without demanding better and expect to be treated as badly in this job as they were on the last.

Well, the Alaska Railroad is using Americans and they are not serfs. They have rights and know they have rights. They want a union because you have job protection with a union. And better wages. Some of the men have families with them in Alaska so that is an extra incentive to treat them well. Then we have socialists, Bolsheviks, anarchists, syndicalists and out-and-out troublemakers in every work crew. The bulk of the workers are hard-working, but the number of political dreamers is significant.

There is also a problem with management. This is an Army project. Overall, the railroad is being built so the United States Navy can have a consistent supply of coal for its ships. To paraphrase President Roosevelt, the Pacific Ocean is now an American lake. To control the American lake, we need a United States Navy that can be in every corner of the lake. In the old days, say, two decades ago, Navy ships and, yes, the United States Coast Guard ships, were all wood and sail. No more. Now the United States Navy and the United States Coast Guard ships are steel and driven by coal. That made the steel and coal industries very happy. The steel industry is even happier now. That's because steel from the East Coast can make it to the West Coast through the Panama Canal in bulk so ships can be built on the West Coast.

But the coal industry is furious. Again, two decades ago, all the coal for the Navy came from East Coast deposits. For Navy ships – and United States Coast Guard ships – in the Pacific, that coal had to come across the country by rail. There were no West Coast coal deposits. Oil, yes; coal no. At some point in time the Navy and Coast Guard will be using oil, petroleum, but right now coal. President Roosevelt understood that and came up with a simple answer: use Alaska coal. So he withdrew all coal lands in Alaska and turned them into naval reserves. Then he pushed for the Alaska Railroad, not to make Alaskans happy but to provide the United States Navy and the Coast Guard unlimited amounts of coal on the Pacific coast. Then the United States Army was put in charge of the project with one goal in mind: get coal to the Pacific Ocean coast as soon as possible.

That 'as soon as possible' got even more important after the Russian Revolution. We now have bonafide revolutionaries working with the ranks of the railroad who want to turn Alaska into a Russian province. We have troops in Siberia to stop that from happening. But those troops will not be there forever. But the 20,000 Japanese troops in Siberia are not going to leave. They are going to drain every possible dollar – or, I guess, Yen – out of Siberia. Then they are going to look west. To Alaska. And Alaska does not have an army to stop them. But we do have a Navy and that Navy is going to need every ton of coal the Alaska Railroad can provide.

Having the United States Army build the Alaska Railroad is like Prohibition. It's a good idea but it won't work. Army personnel have to follow orders, workers do not and will not. Particularly if the order is stupid. People are not going to stop drinking just because it's illegal. Making anything illegal just raises the price. Having the Army in charge is going to cause real problems. Yes, the Army engineers are good. But they are engineers and engineers are not paid to get along with workers. They are paid to lay out plans and then move on. And when you work with engineers, you know they do not have a sense of humor. Sometimes you need that sense of humor to get something done.

But the biggest problem is that the workers you and I have to deal with, are focused on money and safety. This is a great job for them. It pays well, provides food as part of the job and a place to sleep. Even if you have a family it's a good job. But it is a job. When it finishes, they will look for another job. Yes, some will move up to supervisor positions, but for most, this is just a good-paying job. But for the men in charge, the Army men, they are looking for promotion. Particularly with the war in Europe. Those supervisors want to go from Lieutenant to Major to General. Wartime makes that possible. So those supervisors are looking to make a name for themselves, even if it means cutting some quality corners on the railroad.

And that, my friends, is where we are now. We have the Army in charge of a project that should be run by professionals, and it will not be long before the supervisors will be promoted out and young ones will come in. Instead of having hard-core professionals running the construction, it will be new Army recruits, many of whom have never been in charge of anything. What that means for us is we will be spending more time soothing over stupid mistakes by Army personnel than keeping the workforce on track. When the Army is in charge of a military operation, it is efficient. When an army is put in charge of something where workers do not have to take orders – and will not take orders – it is a mess. And that, my friends, is where we are now."

THE SEWARD TERRITORY OF ALASKA, GOLD RAILWAY ROBBERY OF 1926

Late in the Fall of 1926
when the slopes of Mt. Marathon started to pitch
snowflakes by the bushel and sleet by the ton
the city of Seward, a white shroud did become
with all folks locked in from September to June
thriving on moose meat and dance fiddle tunes.

It is said in Alaska, there are only three months --
all starting with a "J" -- and the sun only shunts
from eastern horizon to the sea on the west
rising at ten, all golden in dress
then drops like a stone into the sea
with darkness arriving just after three.

At the end of October comes Halloween day
when the children dress up in any odd way

to tramp from their homes as goblins and ghouls
in masking and costumes, all meant to fool
to secure from their neighbor's candy and gum
while their parents settle in for chitchat and rum.

As the folks of the city slept snug in their beds
with nary a thought of crime in their heads
a plot was unfolding, delicious in scope,
which required some sweat and a smidgeon of hope
to break into the bank and its vault full of cash
and abscond with the loot over the pass.

As Seward was born as a railway town
no buildings had basements set into the ground;
they were modules on flatcars on the webbing of tracks
which had shuttled the structures forward and back
'til the railroad commission established the town
and anchored all buildings firm to the ground.

As June follows May and each Winter a Spring,
summer to Seward incoming cargo did bring,
cargo by barge load as incoming freight
with cross ties by the ton and whiskey in crates,
boxcars of boots and mutton in shank
to be sent northward all the way to Fairbanks.

Year after year, the cargo came in
and the profits grew fatter, never too thin
so the structures on rail were secured to the earth
with concrete and rebar sunk into the earth.
Lawns covered the rails rusting deep in the ground
and docking for barges appeared in the Sound.

As the city grew richer, and so did the banks
transforming their vaults from abandoned planks
to iron and steel with reinforced hinges
and hired armed guards who eschewed binges.
So the burglars abandoned their vault robbery scheme
concentrating on the incoming gold stream.

Everyone knew when the nuggets of gold
would come down the rails with doré whole
from Fairbanks and boomtowns far to the north
where miners were thick as curdling cream. Henceforth
the booty would go 'cross town in a tank
from the boxcar in the station to the five city banks.

There was only place gold was left on its own,
when no one was watching the gift from the loam.
Between Fairbanks and Seward in a boxcar
the security guards were all kept afar
for one could not steal from a moving freight train
so the thieves began a storming their brains.

The scheme that was hatched was both clever and bold
as such was needed to steal a boxcar of gold.
When the freight train came south from northern depots
it was often stalled by the mountains of snow
which covered the tracks coming over the pass
stalling the train until the storm passed.

On the crest of the pass was a spur line left to rot
which, at one time, led to a mine long forgot
which, in its day, produced just enough gold
to spur a stampede. Then, like a bunghole
that quickly goes dry; the rush crashed to a halt
when it was revealed, the strike had been a salt.

But the rail tracks remained, so the cabal had a chance
to switch the gold car before the train could advance
down from the pass covered with snow

to the city of Seward and the banks down below.
The plan was so simple, surprising the four,
was that no one had tried this before.

Thus it came to pass on a blistering day,
when the weather held the gold shipment at bay,
the thieves' plan went forward without a hitch
and the boxcar of gold was for another car switched
and the train less the gold was Seward-bound
the thieves went for the cache while singing a song.

Clearly well known in every small town,

truth and rumor together rebound
from church pew to work site and store to saloon
from the earliest rising to the rise of the moon
and no one is immune from gossip or hoax,
be they well-heeled, religious, or broke.

When the thieves broke the lock on the purloined boxcar
to secure personal wealth in both nugget and bar
they were flummoxed and startled by what was inside;
from one wall to the other and well up all the sides
was a mountain of black rock stacked tall like a shoal
and was immediately identified as a shipment of coal.

It was never revealed how the bankers did know
the boxcar of gold would be stopped by the snow
on the lip of the pass where bandits would snitch
coal instead of gold. So the train pulled a switch
thus leaving the theft as the working of clowns
and the butt of all jokes in old Seward town.

Johnathan Abernathy, Paymaster

M en, whether you are in favor of a union or not, there is one issue you should all take to heart. It is a serious issue. It's scrip, bingles, flickers. Whatever you want to call them.

Now there has been a lot of talk about money lately. I know, what you are being paid, what I am being paid, is not real money. It is just a notation in a logbook. Smaller amounts, like coins and what you might spend if you happen to need some refreshment – which I know nothing about – has to be with coins. But none of the coins are real money. In fact, the ink in the logbook for your wages is a fantasy. As an example, if you have a labor account with the railroad and have earned $500, that $500 does not exist. That is, if you go to the payroll tent and ask to see your $500, they will laugh at you. That $500 does not exist as 500 dollars in gold. But it does exist when the amount is telegraphed to your bank in the Lower 48 states.

Banks are, well, how can I say it, not dependable. Just because your money is in a bank does not mean it is safe. Banks go under every day. Not so much now that they are flush with money from the war in Europe because they have a lot of what is called *equity*. Equity means a lot of people have put gold and government paychecks into the banks. But again, that's not money. It's just paper.

Now, and the reason you are here, is that there is a lot of grumbling that you should be paid in United States dollars. Or gold. First, that is not going to happen because it will mean bringing gold all the way along the line. Then, when you are paid in gold, what are you going to do with it? You can't work with it in your pocket and if you leave it in your sleeping area, well, who knows what might happen to it.

I'm telling you this for a number of reasons. First, you are the luckiest men in the Territory of Alaska. Why? Because the federal government is paying your wages. What this means is that your money is secure. If the federal government puts money in a bank and the bank goes under, you can still get your wages. Second, the railroad is doing all the paperwork to get your money south. If you were in Seward or Fairbanks, you'd have to take the risk of finding a bank in the Territory of Alaska that has a solid connection with a bank in the lower states. You make one mistake, and you lose all your money. Third, with scrip you have money you can use here for whatever things, er, services you want. You won't have to walk about with $30 or $40 in gold. That's dangerous.

So, I guess that's all I have to say. Your money is safe right now. It's guaranteed by the railway and it's guaranteed to reach a good bank in the lower states. It is not reasonable for the railroad to pay in gold and it is not going to happen. I'm sorry if that does not make you happy but that's the way it is. End of story."

Chauncy "Keys" McDoogle, Telegraph Operator

You know, Mr. Tibbs, this is *not* labor well spent. Yes, yes, yes, I know the telegraph is a necessary part of a railway, particularly one here in Alaska, in, quite literally, the middle of nowhere. But that being said, wireless communication has come a long way since the war. I know because I was there. Not the whole time, 'course, but I was there. Part of the Air Corps. Army.

The technology of communication is coming fast. When the war started, that is, when we entered the war, communication with the pilots was by Morse Code. What we're using here on the telegraph line alongside the railroad. By the time the war ended, it was voice communication on the front line. Now there were problems, always are, but over the long run technology works them out. But the big thing here is we, you, the Alaska Railroad, are spending a lot of money on technology on its way out. Every mile of track we lay has a mile of telegraph wire alongside it. That's the way it's been since the Civil War. That was top-of-the-line technology then. Not so today.

Do I have a better idea?

Sure, instead of stringing lines, let's put up some kind of power stations along the railroad line and beam the messages. Wireless, I mean. It will be faster and cheaper. Will the weather affect the transmission? Probably. But if there is a heavy snowfall it will take out the telegraph poles and wires anyway. Yes, power will be a problem along the tracks but the telegraph power needs boosting too. I suggest we stop putting in telegraph wire and put in wireless stations. That way we'll be ahead of the game. And, as the technology improves, we will already have the system in place so we can just trade out the old for the new equipment rather than have to pull out the entire telegraph system."

SEAL

Seal, in both singular and plural, had no knowledge of the primeval. Knowledge of the primeval requires an understanding of history in the sense that yesterdays are different from tomorrows. Human knowledge is based on the reality there is no such place as the 'present' as that delusional instant is simply when the events of the past are transformed into the problems of the future. One does not advance, step by step, into the future. Humans are locked in place and problems from the past bedevil them in the future.

Seal do not have a concept of any of this. Their future is not dictated by what they did in the past, as individuals or species. Their survival is dependent on dodging the problems brought to their world by species unlike their own.

Twenty years earlier, Resurrection Bay off the coast of Seward was just saltwater coastline. Now the throb of steamboat propellers sliced the primeval stillness of the bay. The click, clang, clank, and clatter of the docks being built and the tons of cement and rebar and beams and picks and timbers coming ashore frightened the seal far down the coastline. Then came the barges with construction engines from the Panama Canal, wallowing deep in the waters and occasionally being blown off course by the unpredictable winds.

Then came the filth, the shipping debris and privy overflow. Bottles and cans and crates and cartons and burlap sacks blew or thrown into the pristine waters of Resurrection Bay. Flotsam and jetsam, paper and bottles and cans and barrels and burlap started on the surface and sank to an ignominious fate, left to dance along the bottom of the bay as the currents directed.

With the advance of civilization came the retreat of the fish and crab. As the fish and crab fled, so did the seal. But it mattered not to the landlubbers because what was important was the offloading of the cross ties and rebar and cement and bridges. There was money to be made whether you swung a sledgehammer or drew blue lines on a sheet of paper. It was the opportunity of a lifetime.

But to the seal, it was the end of a lifetime and they moved on.

"Joe Smith," Bootlegger

Marshal! You know better than that! This can't be liquor. You know liquor's illegal in the Territory. Why if anyone tries to smuggle liquor aboard a steamship to Alaska, it gets snagged in Port Townsend where the United States Steamboat Inspection Service goes thoroughly through every steamboat coming to Alaska. With the three men on duty. I hear six ships a day come through Port Townsend and not one drop of liquor is allowed north.

Then, of course, the United States Coast Guard stops whatever liquor it finds on board any ship in Alaskan waters. It must do a phenomenal job of stopping any liquor that slips by the Steamboat Inspection Service men in Port Townsend because there is no liquor in the Territory. We know that because there is the Bone Dry Law here. Look at it another way. How many cases of possession of liquor have you seen anywhere in the Territory last year? Correct none. There you have it; there is no liquor in the Territory.

Oh, you mean the cases of selling liquor to Indians. Well, that liquor must be coming in from Canada because, you know, there is no liquor coming into the Territory because it is stopped in

Port Townsend or by the Coast Guard. So that liquor has to be coming in from Canada. And the white men who sell that liquor. Disgusting people, Marshal, disgusting people. It is illegal to sell liquor to Indians, Natives, and those men should be prosecuted. But that liquor, like I said, had to have come from Canada.

Blind pigs? There are no blind pigs in the Territory because there is no liquor in the Territory. So, there can be no liquor being sold to any work crews along the railroad. There are no blind pigs here along the rail lines, Marshal. Any liquor that appears along the rail lines has to come in from Canada because, you know and I know that there is no liquor in the Territory because it is stopped by the Steamboat Inspection Service in Port Townsend or the United States Coast Guard. And the stories of blind pigs anywhere in Alaska, well, that's just a myth. It has to be because there is no liquor in Alaska because of the Bone Dry Law, so, in a nutshell, these crates labeled peaches are, in fact, peaches and cannot be liquor in any form because there is no liquor in the Territory of Alaska. I swear it."

KAREN WHITTAKER

August 23, 1919

Darling,

I and the girls really miss you. Really miss you. I guess you could say we are blessed you are working on the railroad. Being a professional keeps you in the Territory of Alaska instead of on the front lines in Europe but from what I've heard, it's as dangerous there as in France. Besides that, you're too old to be on the front lines. We all want to be younger but sometimes being old is a gift.

Seward is quite the town. I've never been to a boomtown but this sure is one. There are lots of jobs but more than enough men for the jobs. I can imagine what a cow town in Kansas or Nebraska would have been a hundred years ago. Here the money being spent is by the stevedores and sailors. Teamsters too. The town never sleeps.

We're still in the room at the hotel where you left us. It's too expensive to live anywhere else. Elsie is working as a bookkeeper for a shipping company and Sarah is married. Sam is worried he might be sent to the front. He's a hod carrier, brickman he calls himself. A lot of buildings are going up. Some of them are built for the ages. Out of brick. The rest are wood. That's not a good idea here in Seward. Fires are common and one day the whole city will just burn to a crisp. Steel and cement buildings on the dock will survive and the brick building Sam is building. Jeanette is finishing high school. Has a beau so we'll see what happens.

In one way you are lucky to be on the railway. Right now, prices are going through the ceiling. Because of the war. Everything the Army in the field needs is being sent there. We have meatless days and wheatless days and people are even drinking less. Well, not that much less. Everyone knows Prohibition is coming in a few months so everyone who drinks is filling up before it's illegal. But it will never be illegal. It will just be more expensive, and the police won't be looking for any liquor very hard – unless it's being sold to Indians. Or, Natives as they are called up here.

But there is one nice thing about the war: ration stamps. I don't have to buy food. I just use the government-issued stamps. The word on the street is that the government issues ration stamps so everyone believes the rich are suffering shortages along with the poor. This is the way the government thinks. Actually, it's just a way of keeping the poor and working class from bread riots and meat riots and beer riots like there are in Europe. The rich will always have enough.

Other than that, all here in Seward is as it was when you left six weeks ago. I and the girls – and Sam – look forward to seeing you back here when you can make it. Stay safe!

Love,

Jethro Sandoval, Cement Mixer

C-n-i-d-u-s. No, I do not know how to pronounce it. I'm guessing it's 'snide-us.' It's Egyptian. Rather, he was an Egyptian. A cement man, just like us. Cnidus, smart man. Clever. See, when he was building the lighthouse of Alexandria.

In Egypt!

It's a country in Africa!

What kind of education did you get?

Really? Well, you'd better learn fast because if you want to be successful in life you'd better have an education. I know. Can't go back to school. Then start reading. Don't stop.

I'll give you the background. The pharaoh, that's the king of Egypt, wanted a huge lighthouse in the harbor of Alexandria. Alexandria was the biggest city in Egypt. It had a lot of traffic. Boats, not cars. No cars in those days. Weather was not dependable so the pharaoh wanted a lighthouse to guide ships with cargo. So he ordered this huge lighthouse built.

Cnidus was the architect, and he was a cement man. Like I said, just like us. Cnidus knew cement eroded over time. Just like we do. Cement hasn't changed that much. Some of the cement in Egypt is still around. And in Rome too. But Cnidus knew that rain would erode cement. Slowly, but it would erode it.

What did he do?

Got clever. What he did was chisel his name in the rock foundation of the Alexandria lighthouse. See, there was a rock foundation for the lighthouse and then the concrete, cement, whatever they called it then, went on top. We aren't using rock foundations for bridges here on the railway, just cement. But it will last.

Anyway, Cnidus chiseled his name into the rock foundation and then covered the rocks of the lighthouse base with a layer of cement. Then, clever devil that he was, he etched the name of the pharaoh into the cement. The pharaoh saw his name in the cement and was pleased as peaches. What the pharaoh didn't know but Cnidus did was that over time the salt water would erode the concrete. Long after Cnidus and the pharaoh were gone, the pharaoh's name would be washed away. But the chiseled name of Cnidus would last forever. Lighthouse is gone. At the bottom of the harbor but I'll bet if you swim down you'll find the name Cnidus still on the rock foundation.

Why am I telling you this? Because cement, or concrete, is not forever. Here in the Territory of Alaska there is a lot of water and water does terrible things to concrete over time. It rots. Worse, particularly because we are embedding steel rods, rebar, into the concrete, if there is even a sliver of a crack in the cement, it will let in water. Water hits the steel and starts to rust the metal. Over time, the steel will rust away and down will come the bridge. I'm telling you this because we are being extra cautious when we pour concrete over rebar. It's got to be thicker than, say, in Kansas. Kansas doesn't have earthquakes like Alaska.

Just for your education – which you will get from reading books – the lighthouse became known as the *Pharos*, short for the word *pharaoh*. Over the centuries, the word for *lighthouse* in

European languages was used and in English, the men who operated the lighthouse were known as *farrows*. The family name is still with us today and a lot of Farrows who live in the Midwest have absolutely no idea where their name originated. It's history, son. Read books.

And, no, we are not going to etch our names into the foundation of the bridge foundations we pour. The only place we want our names to be permanent is on the pay we have sent to banks in the lower states."

Jonathan Sanders, Coal Mine Claimant

Curse you TR, President Theodore Roosevelt. You may be dead now but I still curse you for what you did. You and all of the smoke and mirrors over coal land and Naval Petroleum Reserves. I'm just a workin' man and I don't play politics. But I am no fool. What you did, curse you President of the United States, is put me out of business. I owned a coal mine. Well, not the whole mine, just a share of one. When you withdrew lands from the public domain – a fancy way of saying 'Hey, you're out of business!' – I went broke.

I used to have a claim to extract coal. I used to make money selling a product. I had a legitimate entry permit. Then, one day, it was over. My coal land claim disappeared. Vanished. Poof and gone!

But wait! The story does not end there! What happened next was pure, out-and-out thievery by the United States government. I was forced out of the business, but the business did not go away! Now the United States government is tapping the same coal fields for the United States Navy! I'm no fool. That's what the Alaska Railroad is all about: coal for the Navy. Instead of paying me to mine the coal and make a profit, the United States government is mining the coal. Is that legal? Apparently so. Because no court has said what happened was illegal. So here I am, back where I started, as a common laborer and watching while my investment in a coal field went poof and gone. Curse you Theodore Roosevelt. I hope you pay in your afterlife for what you did in this one."

SALMON

Primordial has no meaning to salmon. *Salmon* has no meaning to salmon. Salmon do not think the way humans use the term. They are wild animals and have no concept of tomorrow. Yesterday was hazy. But they do have ingrained intelligence. If a salmon is swimming upstream and a bear is crossing the stream, the fish will swim around the bear. As long as the bear is moving, the salmon will avoid the beast. But the moment the bear stops, the salmon cannot detect the difference between the bear in the stream and a large rock. Which is why bears stand and dine rather than chase salmon.

Fish are not smart in the human sense either. But they do learn to take advantage of changing situations. As the Alaska Railroad crossed streams, cement structures had to be built. Then, as soon as the bridges were built, the workers were surprised to see fish cluster around the footings. Not salmon, other fish. Because when salmon are in fresh water, they only have one purpose: a destination where they will spawn and die. But the other fish would cluster. Finally, a biologist told the Alaska Railroad people the fish had learned that bridges alter airflow over the stream. Insects that used to glide over the stream on wind currents now slammed into the structures. Then they fell into the stream water below and the fish dined.

Salmon did not dine in the streams of Alaska. As fry, they flood the waterways on their way to the ocean. Only one fry in a thousand made the ocean meadows. Five, six or seven years later, the fry that survived the ocean would be back, churning their way upstream to their pool and eddies of their birth. Salmon did not care about the Alaska Railroad. Salmon did not care about the bridges overhead. Salmon did not care about the fishermen on shore or the fish wheels or the salmon drying racks. They are only on a journey to spawn and die and the bridges of the Alaska Railroad did not impede that quest in any way, shape or form."

GERALD "BOWSPRIT" WHITTAKER

Gerald "Bowsprit" Whittaker did not have a dishonest bone in his body. He did not have an honest bone either. He was very much a man of the sea. As such, you lived the wind, shoals, and currents as you found them. Questions of honesty, integrity and compassion were consigned to shorelines. On the water, all was rope, rigging, splicing and Native women when you went ashore.

Bowsprit had started on the New England coast – in more ways than one. First, it was where he had been born. Second, East Coast shipping had been his escape route from personal traumas which had boiled out of control. Third, he preferred the sun, heat and Native women of the Caribbean to the possibility of a jail cell in New Hampshire. Fourth, shipping dollars went further in the Bahamas and Mexico than in Boston and New York.

Fortunately – or unfortunately – he tired of the advance of civilization along every running foot of the Gulf of Mexico. So, it was time to move on. He eschewed whaling because the end of the voyage where he would be paid was in New England which was too close to New Hampshire for comfort. Yes, there was money in whaling, but the voyages were long and had to round

Cape Horn coming and going. The voyage around the Horn was even concerning for the seasoned sailors.

Then came a blessing.

A maritime blessing.

Bowsprit was not there at the precise moment when it happened, but the event was to do three things at the same time. First, it freed Bowsprit from bounding from ship to ship in the Gulf of Mexico so he would not be on a voyage back to New England. Second, it opened untapped seafaring shoreline for his exploitation without having to round Cape Horn. Third, the pay was higher, transportation provided and suddenly he would be as far from New England as he could be and still speak English.

Bowsprit was in a tavern and brothel in Havana when he heard the news. It was news in the sense it was a momentary tidbit of news but, to Bowsprit's point of view, not personally noteworthy. Everyone had known the event was coming. That is, everyone in the sailing industry knew the world was going to change but, then again, the only ones in the shipping industry who cared a pin were the ship owners. For the sailors, well, it was just ship-to-shore tommy-rot.

But it did happen.

At precisely two minutes after two o'clock Washington D. C. time on October 10, 1913, the President of the United States, one Woodrow Wilson, pushed a button on his desk. An electrical pulse running at 670,616,629 miles per hour surged 3,977 miles south to a remote locale in the middle of nowhere now called the Panama Canal Zone – purloined by another President, Theodore Roosevelt – where it detonated seven metric tons of dynamite. The explosion cleared the last remaining division of Pacific and Gulf of Mexico waters. One year later, Bowsprit was on the Pacific without having to sail around Cape Horn.

The Pacific was good for Bowsprit.

With the opening of the Panama Canal, goods from the East Coast of the United States did not have to round Cape Horn. While the transportation of goods to the West Coast from the East Coast may not have been cheaper, the real blessing was goods from the Far East could now make it to the East Coast faster by ship than rail. Even more important, with the outbreak of the war, there was a need to get Far East goods to the war industry in the United States.

But for Bowsprit, the first blessing was Alaska fish. Fish of all species were war materiel and there was an unending appetite to eat in the United States. Fish filled the void of other foodstuffs that were being sent to the battlefront in Europe. Second was the building of the Alaska Railroad. Construction material for the railroad had to be shipped north because there was no rail connection between the Territory of Alaska and the Lower 48 states. Everything for the railroad had to come by ship.

Further, when the railroad opened for business, there was an ongoing need for ships to carry Alaska products from the Territorial Interior to ports on the West Coast. This was still a few years away, but Bowsprit knew he was in the right place at the right time to make a killing as a sailor. Even more important, he did not have to choose which ships he signed onto because no ship carrying construction material to Alaska or fish from Alaska was headed to New England.

Then the best news got better. There was a new Governor of Alaska, Thomas Riggs, Jr. Riggs had spent seven years with the surveying crew which established the Alaska-Canada border. As the United States Engineer-in-Charge, he had firsthand knowledge of the difficulty of keeping an operation – any operation – in the Territory of Alaska supplied. This was more than just a hurdle of distance but greed as well. Shipping goods to the Territory of Alaska was expensive because there was no backhaul. Ships could only reach Fairbanks when the Bering Sea was not covered by ice and the Yukon River was ice-free. Once the ships had offloaded the goods for sale in Fairbanks, there were no goods to be onloaded. So, the ships left Fairbanks empty. Until they arrived at a coal field. Then, one thousand miles downstream, they might be able to pick up a load of salmon but this was rare because salmon canneries already had a contract with shipping firms for the export of the goods.

Because there was no backhaul that was not coal for the Navy – the reason the Alaska Railroad was constructed – shipping companies were reluctant to assign ships to the Alaskan route. If the companies could make better money somewhere else, they would take their business elsewhere. This was often done at the last moment and, historically, frequently. What this meant to the boomtowns north of the Aleutian Islands and up the river watersheds, food and supplies which should have been there for the winter were not. So there was hardship that never should have been.

Riggs was not a fool. He did not live with the problem; he lived with the solution. He convinced the Territorial Legislature to legislate the creation of a fleet of Alaskan ships to exclusively supply Alaskan communities with supplies. This was nothing new to Southeast cities which did not suffer any icebound communities. But for Fairbanks and the communities which would link with the expected webbing of railroad tracks, it was a matter of life and death.

Riggs was also a well-educated man. He knew of and thus could take advantage of a void in the United States Constitution. States of the United States were free to develop roadways or railways within their borders. Regulation of the waterways was the purview of the United States government. But Alaska was a Territory so there were no rules. After all, the Alaska Railroad was funded by the federal government. This could only happen in a Territory because within a state, a federally-funded railway would compete with a private or state-funded railway. This would be a violation of the United States Constitution. But a Territory could have a federally funded railway.

So why not a Territorial shipping fleet? States could not have them. But Alaska was not a state. Alaska also had no waterway border with another state. And if you could have a Territorial shipping fleet, maybe you could even get the federal government to foot the bill.

The residents of Fairbanks were ecstatic about the idea. Their city was a long way from the ports of Seattle and Portland. Even with the construction of the Alaska Railroad, goods from the Lower 48 would still be a long way away. While Riggs could not reduce the distance between Fairbanks and the docks in Seattle and Portland, he could reduce the time necessary for those goods to reach Fairbanks. So, Riggs convinced the Territorial Legislature to approve the formation of the fleet.

And stick the United States government with the bill.

Suddenly Bowsprit was the one thing in life he never expected to be: a bureaucrat. Rather than walking the deck of a whaler with a weather eye, he was pacing cabin floors with pencil and pen to establish shipping contracts for the Territorial fleet. But, in a certain sense, he was still racing the devil. In this case he was not trying to outrun a storm. He was leading the way for a shipping fleet he would command. But his command center would be in Fairbanks. And he did find it odd he had fled one snow country as a youth only to spend his retiring days in another snow country. The only difference was he was now making too much money to pack a carpetbag and flee.

Harry Donahue, Alaska Railroad Track Line Supervisor

Men, men, men. I want to take a moment of your time to set the record straight. Right now there is all this talk of unions and socialism and Bolsheviks. And it is all nonsense because this railroad is not a private business. It is a government operation. Unions are when workers form an organization and that organization talks to management about pay and working conditions, and benefits. That's not going to happen here. The Alaska Railroad is a government operation. Like the Army. In fact, the Army is the management here.

What this means is a lot of workers' terms do not mean anything. You cannot have a union because there is no management. Or, rather, the management is the United States Department of the Interior, and it is a bureaucracy. You all know what a bureaucracy is. It's a way to shuffle off all responsibility on someone else. So, you cannot form a union.

Those of you who are socialists also know socialism is a losing proposition here. Basically, we already have socialism here. The Army, the government, runs everything. You are paid what the Army pays you; you have the benefits the Army gives you, you have the food and rooms the Army provides and you have all expenses to and from work paid for by the Army. The Alaska Railroad is as socialist as you can get in America without a revolution.

Anarchists, and I know there are a few of you, will not work on the Alaska Railroad. The system already exists and is benefiting all of you. Yes, you believe we should be paid more but, frankly, you are working and a lot of people in the Territory of Alaska are not working. Destroying the railroad will put all of you out of jobs. So any talk of anarchism is off the table.

Bolsheviks, same thing. Besides, to those of you who are revolutionaries, the Alaska Railroad is owned by the people. So there is no reason for a revolution. It's already happened. And it was peaceful. If you want a revolution, do it at the ballot box.

The reason we are having this meeting is to make sure everyone understands what syndicalism is. There's been a lot of talk lately about syndicalism and how it should be used for the management and ownership of the Alaska Railroad. So, for a moment, let's discuss syndicalism.

Syndicalism occurs when the ownership and control of a business are transferred to the workers. It is popular in Europe right now and for very good reason. That reason is the war has devastated the economy. So all businesses are small. If you have a company of 10 men mixing cement, it makes sense for the workers to have an ownership role. There is no money to pay them well because, well, there is no money because the countries have been destroyed by war. But syndicalism will be a problem if there were 100 men working for the same company.

For those who are pushing for syndicalism of the Alaska Railroad, it will not work. First, the Alaska Railroad is already owned by the workers. Us. We own the Alaska Railroad already. It is a federal entity and we, the citizens of the United States, already own the railroad. So there is no need to transfer control to the workers, Second, there are hundreds of workers on the Alaska Railroad and all have specialties. It is not as if any one of you can do all of the functions of the railroad. Every one of you was hired for a specific job. You are experts at that job. If you were not, you would not be working at that job. You cannot move someone who is a gandy dancer to a steel worker just because he is a worker. That's a recipe for disaster.

Third, and most important for the talk of syndicalism, the nuts-and-bolts point of syndicalism is to make a business more efficient. The belief is the workers know more about the operation of the business than management. This is true. I would say that the men laying the track know a lot more about the problems of putting down tracks and how to solve the problems of putting down track than the men pouring concrete for the bridge footings. But the men putting down the track do not know how to keep the books, pay the bills, deal with the bureaucrats in the United States Department of the Interior or, in this case, illustrate how syndicalism won't work.

Speaking for management, yes, we know there are problems. There are worker problems, mud problems, bridge problems, accident problems, and a lot of other problems. We deal with those problems every day. Some we solve, others we have to live with. But the most important thing is the railroad is continuing to be built. Turning over management of the Alaska Railroad to the workers is not going to do anything. The same people who are doing their specific job now are going to continue to do the same job. Changing bosses will not change the structure of the Alaska Railroad or the job of the Alaska Railroad. So, if you are a dedicated syndicalist, sorry, it won't work here. After the railroad is built, you might want to form a small company that supports the railroad in some fashion. Then you can deal with their own workers who want to own the company you founded."

BILLY JEROME, MULE DRIVER

With all due respect, sir, it is 1920. 1920! We are in the most sophisticated era of human history. We have a Panama Canal. We have railroads that are already webbing the lower states. We have vaccines for every disease on the planet except the Spanish Flu and that vaccine is going to come fast. Yes, we will, Sir. I have faith in science.

But here we are on the Alaska Railroad, in one of the most desolate places on the planet. There are places in South America that already have railways over the mountains. Yet, here we are, in the Territory of Alaska in 1920 and we are using mules to move wagons.

Mules, Sir! I was on the front line in France for six months and we had our share of mules, yes, sir, but we had mechanized vehicles. Planes and tanks and trucks. Mud was a problem there, yes. But we solidified the roads. Built bridges just like we are doing here. But we were transitioning. We started the war with mules and by the time Germany surrendered, we were using a lot of trucks.

But here, in the Territory of Alaska, with no enemy bombers or enemy tanks or enemy infantry, we do not have any trucks. Everything's coming in by mule. Yes, sir, the railroad is moving slowly but we are ahead of the railroad. We are the ones who are clearing the forest for the rail line the railroad will use. Sometimes we can even see the locomotive moving in our direction. But, sir, we are still up to our ankles in mule droppings. And we have to feed them before we feed ourselves. Sometimes we have to feed them the hay we use for bedding. I mean, sometimes they have more rights than we do and we're the ones laying the timbers and spiking the rails!"

GERALD HARRISON III, CARGO ENTREPRENEUR

Colonel, I'm not going to pull any punches with you. You and I both went to West Point. Just like you, I wear the ring. It's our way of showing the brotherhood. As you know, there is a lot more to the brotherhood than just going to the Academy. We are not only born leaders; we are a unique brotherhood.

I do my homework and so do you so I will get right to the point. Right now, on paper, this railroad is authorized to spend money on the construction of miles of track. The United States Department of the Interior was not specific on the number of miles of track because too much of the Territory of Alaska is wet. Tundra to Alaskans, wetlands to you from the East Coast and swamp to our Academy brethren from the South. The mandate from the Department of the Interior is unclear as to how those miles are to be spent. I use the term *spent* because the mileage is a question of construction expenditure dollars, not one of distance.

Realistically, this Alaska Railroad is not a railroad at all. It is simply the transportation mechanism to move coal from the Alaskan Interior to the coast. Fairbanks is supposedly the destination for the northern end of the railway. But that's just the political angle. You and I know what the reality is. Now, for your reputation and, yes, I will admit I have an angle here, there is a way to salvage the reputation of the Army from future, shall we say, harassment of the appropriation process. Once this railway is completed, there are going to be some politicians in Washington D. C. who will claim this railroad is nothing more than a boondoggle for the Navy. East Coast and West Coast congressmen will disagree with this assessment. The Navy protects the shoreline. But that shoreline is only a concern to East and West Coast congressmen. It is not a concern to congressmen from Iowa and Indiana and Kansas and Montana if you know what I mean.

But, with proper thinking, there is a way to blunt the coming fiscal knives. Once completed, this railway is going to be on the federal dole forever. As money gets tight – and after the war in Europe finishes money is going to get tight – the place to cut expenses if you are representing people from Iowa and Indiana and Kansas and Montana is the Alaska Railroad. Those constituencies do not gain a thing by spending a dime on the Alaska Railroad. Then the budget of the Alaska Railroad gets cut. Cut enough and the rail line goes out of business because, if there is no war, there is no reason to keep providing coal to the Navy.

Now, there is a way to blunt the budget-cutting by those Congressmen from Iowa and Indiana and Kansas and Montana. You must show them there is 'something for them.' There has to be a reason for them to be supportive of the railroad. I have a solution for you to consider.

The best way to get those congressmen on your side is to use some of the miles authorized by the United States Department of the Interior to run an extension of the line into Canada. It will not be costly now that the workers are already on the ground. Extending the rail line to Canada will link the Alaska Railroad with the Canadian rail system. Yes, the rail extension will be a benefit of Canada but only a small one. Canada has no economic power to take advantage of the rail line extension. But Iowa and Indiana and Kansas and Montana do. Now products from those states can be shipped north. Suddenly there will be a new market for their coal and wheat and apples and commercial products.

My suggestion, Colonel, is to strongly support a rail extension into Canada to connect with the Canadian railway system. It will be good for Canada, which will make some in Congress very happy. But the Congressmen who will be far happier will be those who represent the states that are going to try to shut down the funding of the railroad because they do not see a benefit to their constituents. A few dollars spent now on the extension of the rail line into Canada is going to save the Alaska Railroad – and the Army – a lot of headaches in the years to come."

Johnny "Snow Deep and Elbow Grease" Fitzsimmons

I'm from Montana. That's snow country for you men from New Mexico and California. In Montana, we have storms that last days and snow that's five feet deep. But I had never seen snow like Alaska's. In Montana, when it snows on the railway, well, you just plow through. It doesn't pack like it does here. Here the train makes its own tunnel. Or canyon, I guess you could say.

And here you have avalanches. Thick enough to roll an engine! An engine! And I dare say it is the only place in America where you have to get men with shovels to dig a path for a locomotive. That's insane. The point of having a rail line is to plow through snow, to make your own path. But this is Alaska, not Kansas."

PIETRO ANGELINI, CONTRACTOR

You are absolutely correct, Captain. I *am* telling you how to do your job. Let me illustrate it. I grew up in a construction family. Been all over the world. Was in Panama and Italy and Africa working on railroads. But Italy is where this story is coming from. Where I was born.

See, Italy did not become a nation until about the time of the Civil War. America's, not theirs. Theirs was in the same years. All of the city-states became a nation and immediately the rich seized power. So, as far as what happened in all of the city-states was concerned, nothing had changed. Then, when the government, the national government, tried to do something for all of Italy, it was an absolute failure. Why? Because there was too much politics involved. Too many people with their hands in the till.

Russia, where I never was, has the same problem now from the other end. The new government wants to run everything. That is not going to work. I can tell you that right now. What does work is capitalism. By that I mean, keeping the government out of anything that can make money. Regulation, absolutely, but not involved. Once the government gets involved, politics plays a larger role than making the project work. There is wholesale thievery and the rich make money and the workers talk revolution.

What does this have to do with the Alaska Railroad? The Italians have an expression that is appropriate. It is that the government is *Midas a merde.* Cleaned up, it translates as the 'Midas of excrement.' Meaning everything the government gets involved with, turns to, well, excrement.

As long as the United States government is involved with the Alaska Railroad, there is going to be nothing but trouble. Labor disputes will have to be settled in Washington D.C. while the strikers are here in Alaska. Contracts for steel and wood and spikes and concrete are going to be decided in Washington D.C. rather than here where we know the local conditions. Big money in Washington D.C. is going to be calling shots here in Alaska and that is very dangerous when the local engineers are being overruled by muckety mucks in Washington D.C. who have never been west of the Mississippi."

EAGLE

Eagles have a unique place in both human folklore and the wild. They are powerful birds of prey that are associated with dominance and majesty. Spiritually, it is said eagles are associated with rebirth and the coming of a new era in one's life. The bird is also synonymous with endurance and perseverance and to spot one overhead is an omen of success in whatever venture you are currently engaged in.

Eagles are also unique because they are capable of preying on animals which are their own size, sometimes in the range of 15 pounds. They are also unique because of their breeding oddity. Many species of eagles will lay more than one egg. The offspring of the first egg to hatch frequently kills the infant eagle from the other egg and the parents do not disrupt the culling process. Eagles' eyes are twice the size of human eyes and their visual acuity is eight times that of a human.

Eagles were frequent visitors to the skies over the construction of the Alaska Railroad for the simple reason the ground was being cleared for the tracks. This made hunting a lot easier. It also extended the hunting range of the eagles. When there is nothing but unbroken forest, eagles cannot not see their prey on the forest floor. Now that portions of the forest floor were transformed to open spaces, the prey was easier to spot.

But there was a problem.

Just as the ground clutter was cleared, there were no twigs, limbs, branches, and leaves to diffuse the rainfall. Now, when the rain fell, it was a straight shot to the ground. With thousands of years of ground cover stripped away, the soil could only absorb so much water. Rather, the soil absorbed the water and then became mud. In places, knee-deep. While the eagle could soar over the rails being laid, the workmen were not so lucky. Before the crossties could be laid, the ground had to be stabilized. In areas where there were rocks and gravel, it was simply a matter of solidifying the mud with gravel. If the mud was in an area that would not sustain the gravel, like along a creek, ditch or depression, cement had to be used. The cement was expensive, so it had to be used sparingly. But then again, there were so many rivers, gulches, and streams to cross, there was not always enough cement. Or rebar. Cement by itself was not sufficient.

Cement was also undependable. Internally, it was. That is, if the cement footing was six feet deep, the bottom five feet were dependable. Not so much the foot on top. The Territory of Alaska was famous for its rain and every drop caused some erosion of the cement. Enough rain would pock the cement and eventually weaken the footing.

There were other problems with cement as well. In some places, there was no bedrock. This was particularly a problem at the edge of the rivers and streams. You needed the bedrock to guarantee the bracings would not shift over time. Across tundra, the cement was directly on the permafrost. But as the construction crews learned, permafrost is not sold in the sense it is the same at Mile 15 as it is at Mile 231. In the southern portions of the railway, it was in lenses. In some areas it was thick and sturdy. In others, thin like the edge of a plate. Or a glasses lens, where the term originated.

There was also the problem of heat. While the permafrost was frozen soil, the upper crust was not always frozen. During the winter, tundra was frozen from the snow piles on the surface all the way to China, so to speak. But during the summer, the crust of the permafrost was liquid. Swampy would be a better term. Yes, if you dug in the swamp you would hit permafrost. But the problem was not the digging to reach the permafrost to put in the railway footings. The problem was how much warmth the footing would attract from the summer sun. As the footings absorbed daylight warmth, joules of warmth moved their way down into the footings.

Would this affect the permafrost?

No one knew.

If the BTUs did affect the permafrost, would it cause the rail footing to sink?

Or twist?

Would the transformation of the rail line be under just one footing or several?

Or a mile?

No one knew.

All the workers knew was the United States Army engineers said they knew. When you work for the Army, you do what the Army engineers tell you to do.

But there was a problem.

The Army engineers were not Alaskan. They did not have any long-term knowledge of the impact of construction. And some had come from Panama. Alaska was not Kansas and it certainly wasn't Panama.

Inch by foot by yard, the cross ties went down on the gravel and stabilized mud and rock and cement in an engineering juggernaut. It was done the Army way because the Army engineers wanted it done that way and, frankly, by the time there was a geomorphic, geological, geographic or environmental anomaly, everyone who had been present on the construction of those inches, feet and yards, would have long since retired to a place where there was no snow and no mosquitoes.

None of this made any difference to the eagles who soared overhead. The clearing of the forest made hunting easier and a mile or back from the work crews, there was nothing to frighten the eagle's prey back into the forest.

ALBERT ANUNGAPAK

Yes, I know. I don't have to be told. I'm one of the civilized Natives. That's your term, not mine. I know what you are thinking. If I speak English correctly, wear white man's clothes and eat beans instead of smoked salmon, I'm one of you.

It's hard for me to know who I am. I was born in a village whose name you cannot pronounce even if I help you with the wording. Then I was sent to an Indian school in Sitka to be civilized. It was very unpleasant. I was not with my family. I was with other Natives. We were told we were going to be civilized. White. We were going to learn to speak like white people, dress like white people and we could get jobs like white people.

Except we never got the jobs.

But I did learn to think like a white person. The problem is white people make no sense. Even though the Natives have been here for thousands of years, we are still not citizens of the United States.

But now, suddenly, I got a job. Why? Because I don't have the Spanish Flu. And I'm as close to white as you can get – if you are a Native.

Duplicity! A word I learned in the Native school. I am being hired for someone I am not. Or, rather, I am two people and who I am depends on, well, who I am standing in front of.

What? You don't know? Let me explain, Governor J. F. A. Strong made me a citizen. He and the Territorial Legislature. All I had to do to become a citizen was live like a 'white.' This means speaking English, dressing in 'civilized' clothes, eating 'white' foods and not practicing any Native religion. I now have the right to vote – sort of. I can vote on Territorial issues but not federal ones. Which is, as the whites say, a crock because Alaska is a Territory of the United States so anytime I vote in Alaska I am casting a federal vote.

And most duplicitous of all, I cannot drink alcohol. Even though there is a blind pig in every community in Alaska with a population of more than two people, if I buy a drink the blind pig has violated federal law.

There is a change coming. But it is going to take a while. The Alaska Native Brotherhood was established in 1912 followed by the Alaska Native Sisterhood in 1915. It is clear we Natives should be citizens. Full-rights citizens. Not half and half. I mean, why aren't we full citizens under the 14th Amendment? Some of the slaves were Indians. Or Eskimo. Again, duplicity.

But for the moment I'm working on the Alaska Railroad because there was no white man to squeeze me out. But that day will come so I am working now and saving my money. Maybe, in my lifetime, I will be a full-fledged citizen of the United States and the Fourteenth Amendment will mean something to people who have brown skin, eat seal and live in villages with no telegraph lines."

Rufus

No, my name is not Rufus. That's a joke from Billybob. He's from the South. But then you know that. He's got the Southern accent down and remembers all of the old sayings. He grew up in Detroit so I have to guess he picked up the Southern slang from friends along the way.

Now, son, you've never been in the South. You're from California, right? San Francisco? Nice town and everyone's different. When God made the world he tipped it on edge. All the loose pieces fell into San Francisco. The South's different but not the way you think.

Why?

I'm black. Got a lot of words for blacks in the South. But that's not the point. The point is the people in the South are just like the men on the railroad here. A good chunk of 'em think I'm from some jungle in Africa where I spent my time looking for gorillas in the forest. And a good chunk of Southerners could care less that I'm black. As long as I do my job, they don't care. Some folks don't care if you're white like you. Do your job and no one cares. Not everyone will have a beer with you but that's all right. Not a lot of men on the line I'd want to have a beer with anyway.

Most folks don't particular care about your race. People like me stand out because we're black but other than that, we're just like everyone else. Yeah, they are lynching blacks in the South. But there are lynching Norwegians here in the Territory. Just like in the South, two-thirds of the folks think anything to do with race is bad. Just do your job. The folks that don't like you because of the color of your skin are missing the boat. As long as everyone is doing their job, the railroad is moving along just fine. But the minute one man shirks his job, everyone else has to pay. Makes everyone else's job tougher.

I'm just an old guy now, but I was a buffalo soldier. Fought in Cuba with Theodore Roosevelt. He's called TR now but then he was Colonel. Do you even know what a buffalo soldier was? Is, actually, we're still on duty.

See, at the end of the Civil War, many black Union veterans chose to remain in the Army. They were sent west where they became known as 'Buffalo soldiers.' The term came about because of their thick, curly, black hair which was reminiscent of buffalo hair. About 40% of the soldiers in the West were black. And in Alaska. After Cuba, I was a soldier in the streets of Skagway. Never left Alaska. It was District then. Now it's a Territory. And the Buffalo Soldiers are still here. The Territory of Alaska is federal and buffalo soldiers are assigned to protect federal lands. I'm not in uniform anymore but the Buffalo Soldiers still are.

Billybob is never going to be promoted. He can't get everyone to work as a team. I can. I will never be able to convince the Billybobs on the rail line to take me seriously. But there aren't that many of them. Ten years from now I'll be a supervisor because I can get things done. I can make teams work. Billybob spends his time badmouthing people like me. That's fine with me. He's just one less person competing for a promotion and on the Alaska Railroad, you get a promotion for the work you do, not your skin color."

Philip Marengo, Union Organizer

What's the problem here? This isn't the 1890s where you had to fight tooth, nail and shotgun to get a wage increase. That's ancient history. Today it's called forming a union. There is no reason we cannot have a union. We're working aren't we? If we have a grievance, we need to tell someone. Right now there is no one to tell. There is no management. That's the Army way. It's called the chain of command which, right now, does not exist. With the war in Europe, the man in charge today could be in France in a month. Then we have to talk to a new man who might be in France in two months. We've got to have some form of organization here on the rail line because we do have problems that have to be solved."

Harold Donahue, Line Boss

For those of you who keep talking about a union, I have good news and bad news. I'll keep it simple. First, the 'no.' The Alaska Railroad is owned by the federal government, not a private company. A union is an organization of workers who are employed by a company. The union then negotiates with the management of the private company for wages, benefits, time off, medical, whatever. In a nutshell, you workers cannot form a union because you cannot talk to management. I am not management, I am an employee of the United States Department of the Interior and if you demand something, I have to pass that demand on to Washington D. C. About the time of the Resurrection, you'd get an answer.

Now the good news. You cannot form a union but you can – and have—labor representatives who talk to us. Us being management. You have a demand; we will bend over backward to make it happen. If it is reasonable. What we do not want to do and what you do not want us to do is pass along the demand to the United States Department of the Interior. So let's work together.

Finally, as to pay, which is usually the largest bone workers pick, you are already being paid higher than other workers in the Territory. And you are employed when a lot of workers are not. This railway is going to be ongoing for several years, long enough for some of you to retire with money in the bank. So, let's work together to solve problems. You know me and where to reach me. When you have a grip, I have an ear to listen."

DANGERS AND BLESSINGS OF THE EMERGING ALASKA RAILROAD

George Henry, Editor *Alaska Gazette*

There have been many charges leveled against the editor of the *Alaska Gazette*, many of them true. When one becomes the editor of a newspaper, and particularly one in the Territory of Alaska in this decade of political and social upheaval, the slings of arrows of outrageous fortune will be leased. As this is an *editorial* on the emergence of a political and social anomaly, it is important for the readers of the *Alaska Gazette* to understand the position of the *Alaska Gazette*.

First and foremost, the *Alaska Gazette* is the paper of the working man. We are the editorial voice of the workers: socialist, syndicalist and union. Be you socialist, or syndicalist, you are moving America to a better place for labor. Since the Industrial Revolution, the ownership and management of a business that hires labor have skinned that labor alive. Over the last two centuries, the businesses of the world, and the United States in particular, have been in a stampede for profits. And that has been for profits at all cost. Even with the passage of such noteworthy legislation as the Pure Food and Drug Act, you can still find snake oil salesmen aplenty on the streets of America. Laws do not change businesses, only business losses do. So, for the record, the *Alaska Gazette* is the voice of those who are moving nonviolently toward a better America.

In direct response to criticism by many businesses in Seward, Fairbanks, and the growing community on the bank of Ship Creek, the *Alaska Gazette* is NOT the voice of the anarchists or Bolsheviks. Both those breeds of the labor movement are destructive, divisive and dangerous. Anarchists seek to destroy with no thought of rebuilding. The bombing of the *Los Angeles Times* in 1910 is an example. The bombing achieved nothing. It did not advance the lot of the working man. It did not assist in the passage of the Women's Suffrage Amendment to the United States Constitution, and it did not lead to a wage increase or improvement of working conditions in Los Angeles. What it did do was turn the citizens of Los Angeles against labor. This is not productive because our greatest assets are the righteousness of our demands and the support of the people in the street who are not employed by the businesses.

Bolsheviks are equally dangerous to the future of America, labor and business alike. Bolsheviks believe in a world order of workers. This is, on its very face, farcical. The point of capitalism is the expansion of industrialization. The more businesses there are, the more opportunities for employment. Not all businesses are bad and not all workers' demands are legitimate. Russia under the Bolsheviks is failing badly. In the end it will fail. Capitalism, on the other hand, has been healthy and vibrant – with its many flaws—since the Industrial Revolution.

This brings this editorial to a discussion of the Alaska Railroad. It is an oddity. It is not a business, yet it is producing a product. "A product?" readers will say. "What product is that?" The answer is capitalistic. A "product" in a store is a combination of many expenses. To make a shirt there is the expense of cotton. Then there is the expense of coloring the material and the cutting the cloth into swatches to make the shirt. A worker then sews the swatches together. The finished product is put in boxes and sent to market. Stores charge more than the price of the creation of the material. The difference between what the shirt costs the store and what the shirt sells for is called the profit and from that profit must be paid the costs of the heating and lighting of the store, wages of employees and other business necessities.

What is important here is understanding transportation costs are part of the price of whatever you buy. The Alaska Railroad is going to drive the cost of transportation way down. Not just for Fairbanks, it should be added, but Seward and Anchorage as well. Five years ago, cargo to Fairbanks was by a once-a-year barge and, during the rest of the year, horse or mule-drawn wagon. Yes, there was cargo coming in by airplane but it was expensive. Cargo in those days was considered in pounds. A year from now, when the Alaska Railroad is completed, we will be considering cargo in tons. Seward and Anchorage will see bulk shipments coming for the railroad so the cost of goods will go down.

That, of course, is the good news. But there is danger in the future. The Alaska Railroad is owned by the federal government. This means when the workers want to speak with management, that management is in Washington D. C. Worse, management is government employees. Government employees do not think of things in terms of money spent for services received. They only consider if the expense can be covered under the annual appropriation from Congress.

Yes, the *Alaska Gazette* is supportive of the Alaska Railroad. It is good for the working man. It is good for Alaska. It will be good for driving prices down, particularly in the wartime economy that has sent prices skyrocketing. But there is a **caveat** for the working man. Over the long term there is no way to know how working men in a union will be able to deal with management if that management is 4,000 miles away and does not think in terms of dollars and sense for work done.

DANIEL BENCHLEY, WORKMAN

Sir, I'm not an engineer but I have been in Alaska since before you were born. Alaska is not Kansas and you cannot do things in Alaska the way you do in Kansas and expect the same result. I know that I am taking a chance in talking with you, but I do not want it ever said no one told you what is abundantly clear to anyone who has lived in the Territory of Alaska for just one year, freeze-up to break-up.

Right now, someone who is as cunning as a dead pig is proposing to build a bridge across the Tanana River with wood. Those of us who have lived in the Territory can tell you the bridge will not survive the spring. The summer when the bridge is built, yes, it will stay up. Initially, with the freeze-up, the wood bridge will be usable. The ice will form around the timber and hold them in place. But come spring, when the Tanana River breaks, you are going to see river iceberg boulders the size of buildings rushing downstream. Those icebergs are going to smash into the bridge every second of the day and night. It is doubtful those icebergs will break up. What will probably happen is they will form a dam and the Tanana River water will get very deep very fast. This will put unbelievable pressure on the timber of the bridge and down it will come. Come April or May the bridge will be splinters floating seaward.

General Mears knew what he was doing when he built with cement and steel. You want your bridges as high above the water as possible. You want to give the river icebergs as much room as possible to sweep downstream. Anything in the river's path is going to be reduced to rubble. Particularly if it's made of wood.

Will we construct the wood bridge if that's what the Army wants? Yes, we work for you. But a lot of us have lived in the Territory year-round, freeze up to break-up, for decades. We know the power of the river water when it is chockablock with river icebergs. We respectfully suggest the Army reconsider putting a wood bridge in any creek, stream or river in the Territory."

Stanford Pickford, Rail Spiker

I'm not a political man, you know. Yes, I do vote. And I vote for the best person for the job. The best person for the working man, that is. In 1920, I was a strong TR follower. TR for Theodore Roosevelt. He was my man, frankly. He broke from the Republican Party in 1912 and joined with the Progressives. Now **there** was a workingman's party. Not only were their issue righteous, they were a vision of the future. Some future that turned out to be, HA!

Old times, I know. TR got swallowed in 1912 by a Democrat of all people. Woodrow Wilson. Man was more of a Republican than Republicans. The war in Europe made a lot of businesses a lot of money. Not much for the working man and did he dislike blacks! Loved the movie BIRTH OF NATION. Story about how whites in the South retook the South from the blacks after the Reconstruction. He said it was like writing history with a bolt of lightning. Blacks have been second-class citizens ever since. But America should be careful. You can't keep a people down without paying a huge price down the road. It's coming.

Then come 1920, Woodrow Wilson was out. So sick from the Spanish Flu he could not even get out of bed for the last year of his reign. His wife ran it all. First time we had a woman running the country. Then we got the stumblebum in who just died. Maybe died. I think he was poisoned. Had affairs and when he died his wife would not allow an autopsy. What's that tell you about his home life, eh?

Now, he was the first President of the United States I ever saw. Shook his hand too. He was fat and slow, and I have no idea why he was up here at all. For the cameras, I think. Get those photographs so you can run for re-election. But, in his case, there ain' gonna be no re-election.

From the moment he stepped off the steamship in Seward his trip was a disaster. Had a bunch of muckety mucks, secretaries of a lot of departments, and they kind of eased their way up the rail line. Stopped at the coal field in Chickaloon – no surprise there 'cuse that's what the Alaska Railroad is all about, coal – and then on up to Nenana. Now get this, and I know because I was there. The guy in charge of the trip, an Admiral of all people, claimed he knew Alaska. He knew how to spell it but that's about it. He had everyone outfitted with parkas and galoshes and mosquito netting. Parkas in July in the Interior?! When it gets up to 95!? Talk about an idiot! Why they had folks, important folks, passing out from heat exhaustion.

Then he gets to Nenana. Fat ol' President is supposed to drive a golden spike. Not that hard. Not for us who work the railway. But a chore for the President. Governor Bone puts the spike in the right hole and steps back. Harding misses the spike. Misses it again. Finally gets it on the third try. Now the railroad is complete. Started with a woman driving a spike in Anchorage and ends with the President of the United States missing a spike in Nenana.

Then he dies.

With the kind of people advising him, I'm not surprised. He rides the train back to Seward, visits Juneau, goes to San Francisco and dies. Seems his whole life was a stumble forward. Had more affairs than most men have had hangovers and he goes into the ground with no autopsy. Wife got him, I swear.

The only good thing, well, two things, he achieved was driving the spike. It was ceremonial but the railroad is finished. Second, he left Alaska with his muckety mucks. The Alaska Railroad was a typical Army job. Lots of yelling and pointing and politics which you have on the job. The Army is good at getting things done when there is a plan. But getting things done is not the same as running them. Yes, the Army did a good job in building the railroad but, like the President missing the spike twice, the Army just cannot get running anything done right the first time. Or the second time. Until the Alaska Railroad gets someone who knows beefsteak from herringbones, we're going to slogging through a political swamp."

ALBERT FINLEY, TEAMSTER

That's right. We're called teamsters because we drive wagons. With horses. Teams of horses. That's where the 'teamster' title comes from.

You have asked a very important question. It is also not an easy one to answer. Yes, the Alaska Railroad, when it is completed, is going to take away a lot of business from us. Before the coming of the railroad the bulk of the goods for Fairbanks came by barge. But that was only once a year. During the summer when the rivers were ice-free. And some goods came in by plane, but the rest came in by wagon from Canada. The cargo coming in from Canada is still going to come to Fairbanks by wagon. Otherwise it has to be shipped by rail south to Prince Rupert and then placed on a steamship to Seward to be railroaded to Fairbanks. The transportation costs will be too high for that to happen.

But there is a very real question coming. As soon as the railroad is completed there will be cargo by the ton going to Fairbanks. There is no other way for year-round cargo to reach Fairbanks. But we are now in the age of the automobile. Teams of horses are being replaced with trucks. It will not be long before horses in the Territory of Alaska are replaced by trucks. That's a given.

But what is not a given is what is going to happen when an asphalt road is built between Anchorage and Fairbanks. Right now the cargo is going by rail. But that rail is owned by the United States government. It is not a business. Teamsters are a business. Once the road is put in between Anchorage and Fairbanks, the railroad will be competing directly with the teamsters. That's flat-out unconstitutional.

But there's a problem. To use an Alaskan expression, nothing moves slower than a dogsled in deep snow than the federal government at top speed. It will take years for the federal government to stop competing with the teamsters for the cargo traffic between Anchorage and Fairbanks. That's a fight that is coming. Until then, yes, cargo is going to keep coming in from Canada by wagon. Until there's a road for trucks. And that's decades away."

Oliver Harrison, Harrison's Roadhouse Proprietor

A bsolutely I know about the railroad. What kind of a question is that? Everyone in the Territory knows about the railroad.

But I am not stupid. It's just your way of asking a roundabout question. That question is simple: Will Harrison's Roadhouse be put out of business when the railroad is completed?

For the record, since you are a news person, no, we will not be put out of business. Do not look at the railroad as one thing. Look at it as three things. First, it is a shipper of tons of cargo going north to Fairbanks. Second, look at it as a shipper of coal going south to the United States Navy. Third, it is a form of transportation for people who have money.

People who are using the roadhouses now, each one 15 miles from the other, are not going away. People and horses and dog sleds are still going to use the roadhouses. Remember, there is no roadway between Anchorage and Fairbanks. If you do not have the money to ride the train, you still have to use the road-house system.

There are other problems as well. If you are in Fairbanks and want to go to Seward, fine. Take the train from Fairbanks. But once you are in Seward it's a long way from the lower states. You have to take a steamship to Seattle. That's a long way and it's expensive. But with the roadhouse system you can be in Canada and on the Canadian rail system in about 400 miles, the same as the distance from Fairbanks to Seward.

No. And I will bet on that. There will never be an Alaska Railroad link to Canada. Why? Three reasons. First, the Alaska Railroad was constructed to get coal to the United States Navy in Seward. A rail link to Canada is not part of that plan. Second, a rail link to Canada is for merchants to get Canadian goods to Fairbanks. No one in the United States Department of the Interior is interested in helping Canadian businesses make money. Third, the rail link will cost a lot of money and there is no reasonable return for the United States Navy.

So, yes, I will see a decrease in the number of people walking south to Seward. No, there will be no decrease in men walking to the Canadian rail. Maybe there will be an end to the roadhouse system when there is a roadway link between Anchorage and Fairbanks but by then there won't even be bones in my grave to roll over."

MOOSE

Though it is hard to believe, a moose has fewer brain cells than a chicken. Chicken, at the very least, scatter when there is danger. Danger, to a chicken, is anything out of the ordinary. To a moose, there are only two instances of danger: brown bear and wolves. Moose outnumber brown bear significantly and eight months out of the year, brown bear are hibernating. Wolves are a concern but in most cases, they only attack the young and weak. And tales of wolf packs of hundreds are pure fantasy.

Moose have been in Alaska since long before it was known as Alaska. There have been reports in what is now Canada and Siberia since the 1600s. The moose, of course, have no concept of history. Or, for that matter, distance. Moose have a range of a select number of miles and remain in those acres their entire life. It is a life of leisurely browsing broken only by rutting combat of the males and rearing of the young by females.

But now there was a new reality in the forest. And it was pleasant. Rather than trudge through the mud of game trails in the fall and spring and the deep snow of winter, the moose can now saunter down a thoroughfare they had never known before. Moose, being primeval, have no concept of change or advance of civilization. They only knew ease as opposed to slog and the rail line – constructed, under construction and cleared for construction – was an unexpected opportunity to move faster to where they were going.

Not as if a moose knew where it was going.

It also gave the construction crews a chance to change their diet from one of dried fish and beans to one of moose meat and beans. It was a welcome change but came with additional work. Moose meat did not magically leap from bone to cooking pot. There were many stages between and most of them involved sweat, blood, gristle, and stench. But meat was preferred over fish and butchering was a welcome relief after manhandling timber crossties and rail lines.

The moose were unaffected by the change of environment. Even when a moose sauntered by the remains of a less fortunate relative, there was no recognition of luck that the living had escaped slaughter by simply not being in the wrong place at the wrong time. But all humans knew there would come a time when moose mortality would be a statistical note on a log sheet and not cause for a culinary celebration.

SAGEBRUSH BILL

You youngsters! You've got so much to learn. Son, listen to me. No, I ain' your pappy but I'll tell you what your pappys say. I know 'cause I got the lecture in the mines of Bisbee. Arizona, son, Arizona. Hot country. No snow like up here. Lots of sagebrush. Just like my name. Don't use my real one because it would be unhealthy.

Now, here's how it works, son. See, you got to pace yourself. This Alaska Railroad is a good job. Steady job. There's going to be three, four years of a good job. You don't want to lose a job like this. So when you work, you pace yourself. Not too fast because you want the job to last as long as possible. Not too slow 'cause you get fired for that. Just fast enough to stay with the crew. They all know how fast to go. Follow the lead, son. Follow your leaders.

Yes, I know. There's lots of talk of a union. Just might happen because there are no Pinkertons here. No reason for them to be here. This is a government job. Federal money. Flows like a river. No one is pinching pennies, if you know what I mean. Unions are good and bad. They are good because they make sure we get paid what we are worth. We get paid well. There are no strikes. No work stoppage. No work slowdowns. But bad! Let me tell you there are the labor bosses and they are as greedy as the managers. Big money that never makes it to down to us.

So, Son, like I say. Do not upset the crews. Do not work faster than them and do not work slower. Those boys know what they are doing. Been doing it for a lifetime. If you are good, you can d-r-a-g this job out for a lifetime. The railroad is not gonna fire everyone when the last spike goes in. If you're lucky, kiss enough trouser back pockets, you might be employed until the Resurrection. Who knows? Maybe longer."

DANIEL DOMANI, BRIDGE ENGINEER

M en, I have built bridges all over the world. Africa, South America, Panama. All bridges are not the same. Every bridge has its challenges. But I must say, Alaska has brought problems the Alaska Bridge Company has not seen before. Here in the Territory of Alaska, you have mud deep enough to swallow a locomotive, permafrost and rivers where icebergs the size of skyscrapers can uproot bridge foundations.

The Alaska Bridge Company has built a lot of bridges over the years. Made a lot of mistakes and corrected them. This particular bridge is nothing special. It's over a 1,000-foot gulch. 918 feet to be exact. This bridge is what is known as a magnet for photographers. Every tourist from now until the Resurrection is going to be taking pictures of this bridge. It will be the symbol of the Alaska Railroad. So it has to be perfect.

All right, let's go! We are not just constructing a bridge; we are making history."

NORBERT WHITESBURG, ACCOUNTANT

Gentlemen, if you know your history, you know the impact of the fences on the Old West. Fences meant the end of the frontier. Fences meant civilization had arrived. Gone were the cattle drives and in came the farmers. Well, that's exactly what is going to happen when Noel Smith becomes General Manager.

Why?

Good question and from our point of view on the ground, not much will change. But up the chain of command everything will change. So far the Army has been in charge. The military is not a bad administrator when a specific job must be done. Like building a railroad. But the Army is not a good manager. The Army cannot manage. It can command but not manage. Noel Smith is a manager, not a commander.

What kind of changes? Well, first of all, Smith is going for the long game. He will want to make the railroad profitable over the long run, not just in the short term. That means more emphasis on backhaul. It is coal that is making the railroad profitable right now but the Navy is not going to use the coal forever. The railroad must prepare for the day coal is no longer the backhaul.

Smith is also a businessman. He understands the concept of profit. The Army does not. The Army builds with no thought to saving money. It has a budget and it builds to that budget. Smith is a manager and knows how to prioritize a budget. So he is not going to do something that is good for some business but not for the railroad. Like the rail link to Canada. That will only enrich some Territory businesses and never pay for the cost of construction of the line extension.

On and on, Smith is coming in like the fences in the Old West. A year from now, boys, you will not recognize the Alaska Railroad as it was."